COLLECTING CHILDREN'S BOOKS

ART
MEMORIES
VALUES

NOAH FLEISHER
AND LAUREN ZITTLE

Copyright ©2015 Noah Fleisher

Published by

Krause Publications, a division of F+W Media, Inc.
700 East State Street • Iola, WI 54990-0001
715-445-2214 • 888-457-2873
www.krausebooks.com

To order books or other products call toll-free 1-800-258-0929
or visit us online at www.krausebooks.com

ISBN-13: 978-1-4402-4529-9
ISBN-10: 1-4402-4529-0

Designed by Sharon Bartsch
Edited by Paul Kennedy

Printed in China

10 9 8 7 6 5 4 3 2 1

CONTENTS

Introduction

FOR THE LOVE OF THE BOOK
(AND THE KID)

By Noah Fleisher

There is a photograph that hangs in our house of my infant daughter and me (Fiona is 9 now, as of the printing of this book, though I'm a bit baffled how that's happened), taken by my wife, when our girl was a few precious months old. It shows us sitting together, my cheek resting gently against her head – she smelled like sugar cookies when she was a baby and I couldn't get enough of it – as she stares off into the distance. I am reading to her Margaret Wise Brown's classic *Goodnight Moon*.

That picture makes my heart swell every time I pass it. My baby girl, so sweet and smoochable; the book, so simple, profound and readable. I cannot see the oranges and greens of the little bunny's room without being instantly transported back to those early days of Fiona's life (and wanting to say goodnight to a bowlful of mush). When she was born in early 2006, we bought her that book and two others: *The Very Hungry Caterpillar* by Eric Carle and *Guess How Much I Love You* by Sam McBrantney. Neither my wife nor I could have foreseen the journey that was about to unfold for us, a journey that I get to live from beginning to end every single time I look at that lovely little snapshot.

I don't mean the journey of parenting – an adventure unto itself like no other, as many of you reading this can certainly testify to – but, rather, that of the world of Children's Books. Those three simple cardboard books, which we would read countless thousands of times to her, over and over and over – and which would serve as teething toys to her a few months down the line while we expanded her library – were a revelation to both my wife and I.

We read to her from the moment we brought her home. I mean it. Within an hour of her introduction to the apartment where we lived, she was in my lap listening to that baby bunny in *Goodnight Moon*. What followed those first few weeks and years were more children's books, some classic, some not-so classic. It didn't matter. My wife was a ravenous compiler of book piles carted out from the local library. She stored the titles away in her database of a brain; we read hundreds of pages a week.

Now Fiona devours fiction and non-fiction tomes by the dozens: chapter books, kid magazines, comic books, picture books, you name it. In fact, when she was a bit younger, on those occasions when she would need a little discipline, there was one quick "punishment" that would make her see the light: a quick threat to take away her books. Worked like a charm every time.

The bonus of all this is that our kid loves the written word and reads like a champ. What's more, my wife and I reconnected with the joy of reading all the classic titles and authors of childhood again. Very quickly, as you might imagine from a household steeped in antiques and collectibles, we began to realize a burgeoning expertise in the form. We marveled at the compelling simplicity of Eric Carle's various animals, fish, birds and bugs. We loved the messages in Margaret Wise Brown's direct and lovely prose. A. A. Milne's Winnie the Pooh proved every bit as lovely and deep as he did when we were little, and the rhymes and lessons of Russell Hoban's Frances the Badger are the axiomatic backdrop against which we measured our daughter's social progress.

As she's grown, we've moved into the great chapter books for kids, both old and new. We all love Beverly Cleary and her various tales of animals, boys named Henry, girls named Beezus and Ramona and a mouse who has a few amazing adventures on a motorcycle. Her introduction to Mary Poppins, Peter Pan and Willy Wonka were not on the big screen, as they were for me, they were via the various volumes that bear those names and the genius authors and artists that imbued them with life. Last year we visited Frances Hodgson Burnett's *The Secret Garden* and were thoroughly enchanted with the unapologetic magic of Miss Mary, Dickon and sickly little Colin. I can even bear the repetitious adventures of *Humphrey the Hamster*, *The Rainbow Fairies* and the *Magic Tree House*, among so many that she reads for brain candy just because when Fiona wants to relax this is where she goes. It beats any video game or TV show by a mile.

My wife and I are not unique in this immersion in Children's Books. Our generation, a bridge generation between the pre-digital "dark days" when we were forced to read books and the current overkill of the Web in providing every detail of every day in the ones and zeroes of Google, Amazon, Instagram and the like. In fact, it has seemed to us, if anything, there has been a trend back toward a more simple engagement with the written page since the world has moved mostly online. I know we hunger for it and seek it out wherever we can. I know we have friends who are the same.

Given my longtime relationship with the good folks at Krause Publications, and my history in the antiques and collectibles business, it was a short leap to creating this book. When editorial director Paul Kennedy and I started talking about this book, we both felt the time was ripe. It's easy to covet the first and best editions of these books, to see them in their original glory as presented to their first lucky readers.

So it is, then, with love in our hearts and pride in our work that my wife Lauren and I present to you this volume. May it inspire you to re-connect both with those books that take you back to the early days of your own child's life, but also to the early days of your own, to bedtimes and downtimes spent curled on the couch, or snuggled under covers, adventuring throughout the world with your favorite characters. I hope you see more than a few books in here that transport you right there. I know so many of these do just that for me.

What follows are our best efforts to quantify and qualify what it means to both love and collect children's literature. It's about story and philosophy as much as it's about material culture. We have looked at what it means to collect first edition classics, signed and unsigned, from the great names of the past. We have attempted to define the best of the various eras in Children's Literature that populate the 20th and early 21st centuries. We have come to realize – and I hope you will forgive us any oversight as concerns any title or author you or your kids love – that to completely explore this topic would require an encyclopedia of many volumes. We've had to make choices based on the information and images available to us. We apologize to so much of the great Children's Books of the 19th Century that we simply could not cover; the topic is just too vast to sum up in these pages.

While not necessarily meaning this intro to turn into a love letter to my dear daughter Fiona, it's impossible for me not to write this essay – and this book – without it turning into just that. This book, the entire journey, would have been impossible without her. If you're reading this book right now, if my words mean anything to you, then you're thinking about your own children, about their journey through the books they loved so much – and that you read over and over and over to them – and you're composing your own love letter to them, whether grown or growing.

Indulge me, then, as I dedicate my work on this book to her. Fiona, you have been present in my heart with every key stroke. Your father loves you very much, kiddo. Never ever forget that, okay?

MY FAVORITE CHILDREN'S BOOK

While the written word has largely become my life as an adult (both professionally and personally, for enjoyment) I was not a kid that read too terribly much, nor do I have a tremendous amount of memories of being read to by my parents – a forgivable thing, considering that they wrangled with three boys every day, all of us just a year apart and my two older brothers such hellions that I imagine they just wanted a few minutes of peace at the end of the day when we were all finally safely carted off to bed.

It wasn't until I was in college, in fact, that I began to take extended refuge in the printed word. When it came on me, however, it came in a flood and I wolfed words by the tens of thousands. I do, however, clearly recall my favorite book from when I was a small boy. It was called *Jerome*, written by Phillip Ressner and illustrated by Jerome Snyder (Parents Magazine Press, 1967). It's long been out of print and I would doubt there are 10 people reading this book that have ever heard of it.

I don't know how this psychedelic little book came into our house when I was a kid, or why, but it had a huge impact on me and, since it is neither famous nor collectible and will not appear anywhere else in

PAGING THROUGH CHILDHOOD By Lauren Zittle

When our daughter Fiona was born, long-forgotten memories hidden away in my brain were re-awakened. As I whispered the words of *Goodnight Moon* and *The Very Hungry Caterpillar* into her little ears, I recalled my days as a young book worm.

I grew up in the 1970s, the only child of divorced parents. Television was a central figure in my daily life. Thankfully, early on, my mother introduced me to the wonders of Maurice Sendak. *The Nutshell Library* and the *What Do You Say and Do, Dear* books are forever imprinted on my brain. She introduced me to Cricket Magazine, which I vividly remember reading, contentedly curled up on the Murphy bed in our tiny Santa Monica, Calif., apartment.

My long, hot summers were spent in Scottsdale, Ariz., with my father and his family. These days were punctuated by regular trips to the library with my step-mother. One of my fondest memories of this time with my father is of him reading the Dr. Doolittle series to me before bed, the very copies he had read in his childhood.

Clearly, there were many adults involved in making me a reader. When my third grade teacher, Mrs. Ellis, read *Pippi Longstocking* to my class, the adventures of this wacky young girl captivated me. By the 4th grade, I was fully immersed in the world of children's literature. I read everything - from *The Phantom Tollbooth* to *The Borrowers*, from *The Chronicles of Narnia* to everything written by Judy Blume. I named my dog Rontu, just like Karana did in Scott O'Dell's *Island of the Blue Dolphins*.

Flash forward to 2006. I now had a little future reader in my arms. I couldn't wait to share all of my favorites with her.

This journey with my daughter has helped me realize just how much I adore children's literature. I'm inspired and moved by the authors and artists who choose this profession, how they connect with their audience, remembering what it's like to be a kid, just as it helps me to remember.

When it works well, it's magic. It contributes to my parenting and helps me stay connected to what my daughter is thinking. Through this sharing I'm able to guide Fiona to read what's appropriate for her age. I also get the chance to read works that I had only seen on TV, or in the movies, as a child. My husband and I have relished finally getting to read works such as *Mary Poppins*, *Peter Pan* and *The Rescuers* and, in turn, use them to have great family discussions. There have been many a special moment finishing up a book with Fiona running to get me a tissue.

When my husband asked me to collaborate on this book, I jumped at the chance. The opportunity to delve deeper into children's literature has been a joy. Despite being married to a man who works in the antiques and collectibles industry, the idea of collecting had never really appealed to me. Now I realize I have the beginnings of a collection. My shelves hold many old and well-loved copies of books inscribed to me from grandmothers and grandfathers, aunts and uncles, to my parents from their relatives. Collecting is a labor of love, a connection with the past. I can see that now.

As I look at these "real" collections I am stunned. Browsing through the treasure troves of books on the auction block has flipped a switch in me. The idea of owning a signed first edition of *Mary Poppins* now makes me swoon.

"There are perhaps no days of our childhood we lived so fully as those we spent with a favorite book," wrote Marcel Proust.

I hope, as you peruse this guide, that it fills you with love and wonder for this medium. Never before, in this mother's opinion, has it been so important to keep this tradition alive.

WHAT TO LOOK FOR WHEN BUYING

When it comes time to collect, it's important to know what you are looking for. In the beginning, it may be enough to simply get any copy of whatever book you want, or stumble upon in your travels. Even so, becoming an educated consumer is the best thing you can do for yourself and for the people you do business with. It's imperative to understand what you are looking at so you can negotiate the best price, or understand why a bookseller cannot move on their price.

In that spirit, some things to look for as you transition from reader to collector:

The condition of the cover is everything. A description is great online but trust your eyes. How does a book look to you? Does it seem to match the description online or in a catalog? There is a vast difference between a book in Fair condition and Very Good condition.

Does it have a dust jacket? Is it the original dust jacket? Original dust jackets can sometimes mean the difference of hundreds of dollars for a book.

What edition is it? First? Second? 20th? What printing of that edition is it? This, too, can make a significant difference in the value of a book. The edition information is always on the copyright page, listed toward the bottom. Know what you're buying!

Is the spine of the book broken? Cracked? Faded? How about the cover? The price you pay will reflect all these things. It's best to know what similar copies have sold for.

How are the pages of the book? Without handling a book, you cannot determine if there is foxing (age-related spots or browning) to pages, or water damage. Perhaps the pages are torn, or missing. All these things make a difference in the value of a book. If you are not buying it in person then ask these questions in advance. It will show you know what you're doing and make sure you are getting the best book for your money.

Is the book you are looking at the one you want? Does it match with the image you saw online, or the copy you saw years ago, coveted, but didn't pull the trigger on? Condition issues can be overlooked if it's the volume that you know you want and are willing to pay for. Remember, you have to live with the book, and with the price you pay.

If the book is signed or inscribed, and you are paying a premium for it, then you need to make sure the signature is real. Any dealer or auction house worth their salt is going to offer assurances on this, and/or third party authentication, along with further assurances that your money will be returned if you find out later that a signature is false. If this is not part of the deal, then back away. Fake signatures are more common on more popular and famous books, so look carefully. An online search can usually give you a good sense of an author's signature and, with experience, you will soon know right away what's what and who's who.

this book, I would like to share it with you. The copy you see here was given to me by a friend in the months before my daughter's birth. I mentioned it in a passing conversation and she, without me knowing, found it online, ordered it, and within two weeks placed it in my hands.

Jerome is an odd and ambiguous little story, beautifully illustrated and probably not too terribly well-written. It follows the title character's journey one day as he is sitting on a lily pad catching flies to eat. He sees a witch passing by and, in simple observation, remarks upon what an ugly old witch she is. The witch reprimands him, telling him that it's not nice to call people witches and, while inferring she could cast a terrible spell on him, says that, instead, she is going to make him a prince.

She does so, without fanfare of any kind, and tells him to go do Princely Deeds. Jerome himself seems nonplussed by it and, in fact, is unchanged in appearance. It's obviously a trick, but Jerome is un-phased. He marches off to the closest town and introduces himself to the skeptical and laughing townspeople as the Prince that does Princely Deeds.

Mocked at first by the townspeople, who see only a frog, he is finally assigned a Princely Deed: Slay the giant crow that is eating all their corn crops. Jerome accepts the challenge and off he goes to confront the big black bird. As it turns out, the giant crow is gobbling all the corn out of fear of not having enough for himself. After all, who could resist such juicy kernels of corn? Jerome assures him that he himself does not like corn, that he knows many animals that want nothing to do with corn and that all the crow needs to do is share with the townspeople and there will be plenty for everyone. The crow, satisfied, flies off.

In doing two more Princely Deeds for the townspeople – convincing a fire-breathing dragon to work at the town dump incinerating rubbish instead of burning maidens and tricking a cruel wizard with crazy psychedelic green glasses who gets whatever he wishes for into turning himself back into the carefree boy he once was – they come to venerate Jerome, convinced he really is a Prince. They reward Jerome with a little castle, right by a pond with lily pads, where he can sit all day and catch flies to eat.

Just looking at the artwork of this book, feeling the board covers and the thick, treated paper, I am overwhelmed with nostalgia. I can smell the yellow sunlight and dust in my room as I read it sprawled out on the carpet. It is a powerful thing, this little book. *Jerome* spoke to me because I felt, like him, that I had goodness in me. That I had the capability to help and to create change though I might not have seemed it to those around me.

In the end, Jerome solves the problems with brains – not brawn – and realizes his true potential to be, without a doubt, a fine prince. I'm no prince, but I do believe in brain over brawn, any day, and I do believe in everyone's realization of their true potential no matter how they look or what anyone may think of them.

ON COLLECTING

Both Lauren and I have understood, since we started working on this project, that it would be impossible to cover *every great children's book*. Somewhere in here, we are sure, one of your favorite books is missing. While we apologize for this – some of our favorite books are, too – I would remind you that this book is not an encyclopedia, at least not yet.

What it is at its heart, besides a trip through time and childhood, is a book about collecting. Hopefully more than a few people who have no experience in the collecting marketplace will see something that piques their interest and decide to pursue it further. That is the very essence of collecting: pursuing something because it *speaks* to you.

Values and value ranges have been assigned to most of the images you'll see here, and they have been culled from auction results. They are not meant to be a strict price guide that stridently quantifies every dog-ear and split spine. There are variations on first editions, first printings, signed volumes and author inscriptions – all things that can affect the value of a given book. What we have set out to do in these pages is to give you a sense of what you can find out there. In many cases the books presented here would go for more than suggested, and in many cases less. It has to be about the chase, because, as stated above, it *speaks* to you.

Collecting is an emotional pursuit. Ask any expert and they will tell you, if you don't love it, don't go after it. This holds very true with children's books. If this book is your entrée into the marketplace, congratulations and have fun, but make sure you do your due diligence when it comes to buying.

Get to know dealers and collectors, find shows and auctions and attend them. Ask a million questions. Any good auctioneer or dealer will be happy to spend as much time with you as you are willing to spend. Their level of accessibility will rise with your interest and enthusiasm. If you don't love it, don't put money into it – that is the bottom line. The best examples of first edition children's literature, where the biggest names are concerned, is still a competitive market and one that requires a solid foundation to make the right choices.

Meanwhile, however, at the lower and mid-levels of the market, there are simply a ton of great books waiting to be discovered, and for cheap.

If a collector is focused, willing to invest the time to learn what's out there and what to pay for it, there's a broad world of charming books awaiting.

We also had to ask ourselves the question as to whether the massive shift toward digital everything in the last 15 years has affected collectors, and the answer is: certainly, for better and for worse. Things like the iPad, Amazon and the proliferation of video games has certainly punched the rare book market in the gut, but it's no knockout.

On one hand, technology has leveled the playing field and made clear, for the most part, who has what book and where it is – that's a positive. The negative is that there is now a second generation that has been raised in an almost exclusively digital manner and there's been a fall-off not only in the amount of people actually reading physical books, but also in the amount of people seeking out the classics for their kids in any format.

The positive to that negative? There's so much more available to the dedicated and intrepid collector and prices are much more uniform across the board. It's also easy to see now an emerging backlash movement against digital life. In a few generations we may well see a concerted movement back to the printed page, a mid-21st Century revival countermanding digital media's pronouncement of death upon print and making you and the collection you are lovingly putting together look that much better to your children and grandchildren.

What do you then look for in your first edition children's books? Besides the titles you love?

"Three words: Condition, condition, condition," said James Gannon, Director of Rare Books at Heritage Auctions. "Does it have its original dust jacket? Is it signed or inscribed? Is it in good shape or is it torn? Is the hardback cover in good condition? Are the corners bent

HOW TO GET A SIGNED BOOK

Whether you are a collector or simply a fan, getting an author to sign your book can make a world of difference, both in the sentimental value and in the financial value. Getting a personalized inscription – along with a drawing, when possible – can turn the most ordinary book into a true treasure.

Throughout this book you will notice signed and inscribed volumes, many of which have been made much more valuable because the owner took the time to seek out the author and the author took the time to make it special.

The modern age makes it simultaneously more difficult and easier to get a writer to sign your book. It's tougher because the world is wide and full of big cities. You can no longer simply go to a writer's hometown, seek them out and ask for a signature. Authors may also hide behind the firewall of a publisher, making direct contact impossible. Conversely, it's easier because technology has made the world smaller and finding a writer, or a way to gain access to a writer, is just a mouse-click or a book tour away. You just need to have a plan and a little patience.

Know your favorite author has a new book coming out? Usually new releases are accompanied by a book tour through major cities. If you live in one of these places, keep a close eye on the author or publisher website for upcoming dates.

Many authors have websites dedicated to news about their work, announcements and dates of appearances and, if you're lucky, an email address.

Taking a shot and reaching out, in the spirit of respect and appreciation, can have results Most authors worth their salt will write back and, if you ask politely, may send you a signature or provide an address or P.O. Box where you can send your book for inscription.

Publishers are a great resource for gaining access to writers, though it can be a little disconcerting to send your book off to an author in care of a publisher in a big city, where you have no idea who may be handling your request. You have to have some patience and some faith in this case, as it may be a while before you get your book back. A call to a publishing headquarters is immensely helpful and can help you identify the right person to send it to and let you know if they can even get the book in front of the author.

ALWAYS include a return envelope and return postage. It's a sign of respect for an author's talent and time. If you are asking for a drawing, and aren't sure, it's not a bad idea to include an honorarium ($50 or so) as another sign of respect for their talent. Not all writers are making a mint off their books – many work hard to get by just like you and me – and they may appreciate the gesture. They may also send it back to you with their thanks. Always err on the side of discretion and respect.

Your local bookstore can be a great resource not only for letting you know what authors are coming through and when, but they may also have signed copies from a specific author from a previous visit. It never hurts to ask!

COLLECTOR RESOURCES

The websites, dealers and auctioneers listed below are an excellent resource not only for acquiring books, but for educating yourself about the state of the market and the prices that many titles are currently bringing. You'll pay more via a dealer, sometimes significantly so, but you're paying for ease of access – a professional dealer has stock on-hand and access to writers and publishers that you don't, so don't begrudge them the extra money for their effort if it means enough to you. Taken in total, some time well spent on the sites below will go a long way toward introducing you to the range of material, and prices, in the modern market for antique children's books.

AUCTIONEERS:

PBA Galleries: **www.PBAGalleries.com**
Dreweatts Bloomsbury Auctions: **www.Dreweatts.com**
Quinn's Auction: **www.Quinnsauction.com**
Heritage Auctions: **www.HA.com**

WEBSITES:

Abebooks.com
Alibris.com
Ebay.com
Bookfinder.com
Thriftbooks.com

DEALERS:

AlephBet Books: **www.alephbet.com**
Old Children's Books: **oldchildrensbooks.com**
Between The Covers:
    betweenthecovers.com/btc/category/Children
The Antiquarian Booksellers Association of America: **ABA.org**
Bauman Rare Books: **BaumanRareBooks.com**

or shredded? Are the pages dog-eared? Does it have all the pages in it and, most importantly, does it say 'first printing' on that title page?"

The Auction Archives at PBA Galleries in San Francisco (PBAGalleries.com), Bloomsbury in London (Bloomsbury.com), LiveAuctioneers.com or Heritage Auctions (HA.com) are a good place to start any search and to get a good sense of price and condition. Mainstream booksellers like Barnes and Noble, Half-Price Books and Powell's Books (out of Portland, Ore.) all feature good first edition children's books and can give you a good idea of what retail is on a given title. Smart collectors, or would-be collectors, are all also well-served to check out online booksellers like Alibris.com, Biblio.com and Abebooks.com.

All and any of the above are enough to give you a sense of what's out there and, hopefully, a good bead on that signed first-edition Harry Potter you've been coveting since your kids starting reading the books.

A last word of advice from Gannon to the neophyte: This is a true buyer's market right now.

"In the end, I would urge any new collector to find a dealer or an auctioneer that you trust and have a good rapport with," said Gannon. "There has been, and will continue to be, a proliferation of small auction houses selling collections of good books. This is a side effect of the closing of so many brick and mortar stores due to current market conditions."

This means patience, it means not rushing out immediately and buying from the top auctioneers and dealers in the field as they tend to the expensive side. A good relationship with a reputable dealer is very desirable, but there are many tools available to speed along an education.

"Go find offerings that others are missing," said Gannon. "With a computer you can do this from home mostly by looking at auctions and specialty sites and using want lists and keywords to get what you want. The fun comes in getting a great kid's book before anyone else and paying much less for the effort."

SPECIAL THANKS

This book would not have been possible without the patience and help of many people and great minds. Thanks are due to so many of them that it would be impossible to list them all here, but a few special exceptions must be made for a few good folks: Paul Kennedy and the talented staff at Krause Publications, PBA Galleries in San Francisco, CA, Sharon L. Gee at PBA Galleries, Justin Benttinen at PBA Galleries, Heritage Auctions, James Gannon, Steve Ivy, Jim Halperin, Greg Rohan and Paul Minshull, Catherine Saunders-Watson, Harold Hanson and photographer Greg Kopriva. A special thanks to Eric Bradley for his help. An extra special thanks to all the adults – our parents, extended family and family friends, along with all the amazing librarians and teachers along the way – who fostered the love of reading in us both. A final thanks to our daughter, Fiona, without whom we would have had no reason to start this journey in the first place.

IDYLLIC BEGINNINGS
(1900-1919)

he history of Children's Literature and picture books certainly goes back further than 1900. You'll notice more than a couple books in this chapter dating their origins to the 1800s and, in a few instances, even further back. Even so, it is during this amazing era of human innovation and exploitation that the idealized childhood we associate with the Golden Age came to be.

The world at the turn of the 20th century was complex, to say the least. Rapid industrialization was bringing wealth to many like never before, while at the same time poverty spiraled out of control. It was in this clash that the stylized, genteel idea of childhood was born – perhaps in reaction to the times. Those who could afford it took full advantage of it.

Producers of published material, aided by advancements in printing technology, seized this idea and put it into mass printed books that reached through the upper classes – where a leisurely childhood was more available – and into the emerging middle class. The mass-produced picture books and storybooks were a luxury, for certain, but they were not priced out of reach. The result was, in word and deed, magical.

What emerged was fantasy, fairies and epic poems. It was a time of amazing artists, some of the biggest of their day – Jessie Willcox Smith, Arthur Rackham, Edmund Dulac, Maxfield Parrish, to name a few – all contributing to the idea and look of what being a child meant: flights of fancy, natty clothing and the idea that magic was always close and the real world very far away. Books for children measured a future of possibilities uncharted, all while reinforcing polite behavior and gender roles.

It was an age of timeless storytellers, too. Cultural mainstays like Frank L. Baum's *Wizard of Oz,* Beatrix Potter's *Peter Rabbit,* Palmer Cox's *Brownies* and R.F. Outcault's *Buster Brown* were phenomena and rank among the first great American Pop Culture icons of the 20th century. Arguably, the era peaked and concluded with the publication of J.M.

4 COLLECTING CHILDREN'S BOOKS

Barrie's *Peter Pan* in 1914 (following his play, *Peter and Wendy*, which premiered in 1904), a book that remains intriguing and compelling today, and one whose "hero" broadly reflected the just-beginning conflict of the First World War.

Things did indeed turn uniquely sinister with the outbreak of war in the summer of 1914, and the Golden Age came to a quick end. The idea of an idyllic, safe world was shattered; entire nations were forced to grow up almost overnight. A world recovering from a mind-boggling conflict, one whose political repercussions are being felt even today, had no room for fancy. Production of great works for children all but died when the Austrian-Hungarian Empire declared war on Serbia and it would be a good few years after the war's end in November of 1918 before the market in children's books would pick up again.

The whimsy of early 20th century children's books was a reaction to and against the shrinking world its creators inhabited and against the rising tide of uncertainty that would engulf the Western Hemisphere in World War I. These works would inspire the next generation of great children's authors and artists, 1920-1939, a wave of creative minds that experienced the joy of those early modern childhoods but who were called upon at the end of that youth to fight a war that would claim, in all, 15 million lives, destroying the sense of magic they once held so sacrosanct.

These conflicting experiences and sensibilities – gentility vs. brutality – would directly influence the work they created, gifting posterity with some of the greatest children's books of all time, and set off a process of evolving awareness in the writing of children's books that would impact the next century of authors in profound ways.

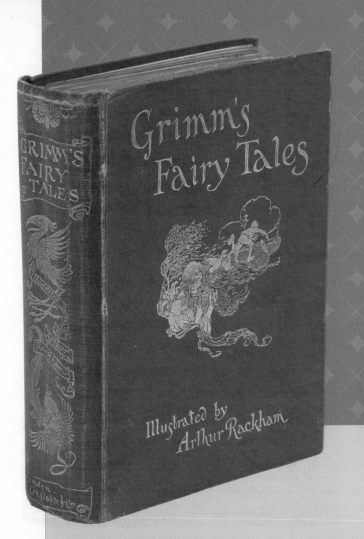

Grimm's Fairy Tales – Illustrated by Arthur Rackham
Constable and Co., London, 1909.

Translated by Mrs. Edgar Lucas. Illustrated by Arthur Rackham, including 40 tipped-in color plates. First Trade Edition. Some of the world's most popular fairy tales, fabulously illustrated by Rackham. **$480** at auction.

Image courtesy Justin Benttinen/PBA Galleries

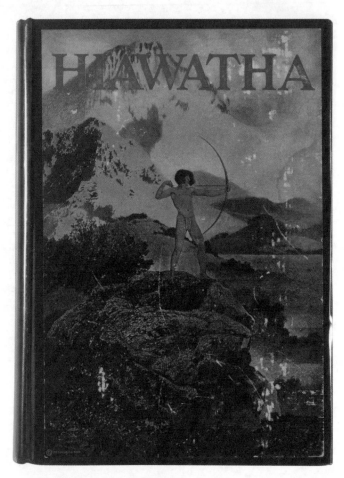

The Song of Hiawatha

by Henry Wadsworth Longfellow, Frederic Remington, Maxfield Parrish, and N. C. Wyeth, illustrators, Boston: Houghton Mifflin, ca. 1911.

Second Edition. A Who's Who of early 20th century illustrators bring Longfellow's classic poem to life — an amazing grouping of talent. This very good copy brought **$62**.

Image courtesy Heritage Auctions

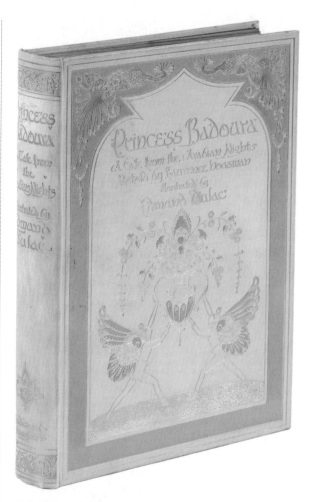

Princess Badoura:
A Tale from the Arabian Nights

by Laurence Housman, illustrated by Edmund Dulac, Hodder and Stoughton, London, 1913.

Delightful illustration by Dulac, equaling, and perhaps exceeding, his Edwardian rival Arthur Rackham with his gorgeous rendering of old Persia. Purchased online for **$510**.

Image courtesy Justin Benttinen/PBA Galleries

Peeps into Fairly Land: A Panorama Picture Book of Fairy Stories

Introduction by F.E. Weatherly.
London: Ernest Nister, circa 1895.

First Edition. The delicate full-color chromolithographed pop-ups in this book are complete and in perfect working order, a must-have that makes this an irresistible copy of this classic in the history of children's pop-up literature. At **$598** in an online auction, expect to pay in the same range should you find one in good condition.

Image courtesy Heritage Auctions

"Well, not always," said the fairy, "but come along!" She opened a little golden door and they passed through it, and there they were, all in a minute, in Fairyland.

It is always mid-May in Fairyland, the fields are always green, and the hawthorns always white, and the buttercups and daisies a-growing, a-blowing; and in this pleasant place the fairy-tale people live. "That's the way to Elfin Town," said the fairy, pointing to a smooth road leading between green meadows. And before they could answer she was gone.

The two children walked along, picking the cowslips and lady's-smocks as they went. Nina's flowers kept fresh and sweet. But directly Noel plucked a flower it changed into a paper one, with no beauty and no scent at all. They had not gone far when they saw something coming along the road towards them—a sort of procession of people brightly dressed. The children stood back to let it pass. But to their astonishment the leading person in the procession stopped in front of Nina, bowing low. It was the Knave of Hearts, and he had a dish of tarts which he offered to the children. Nina took one—it was delicious, but when Noel took one it turned to a little bit of snow and melted in his fingers. "How horrid!" said Noel. "That shows it's a dream!"

"Nonsense," said Nina; "why, mine is lovely. It tasted of raspberry jam and almond iceing."

Then came Puss in Boots, and Nina stroked his furry white head, but the pussy would have nothing to do with Noel, and scratched him quite hard. Noel really hardly knew what to think. Boy Blue came by and blew a blast on his horn that nearly deafened poor Noel. And little Red Riding Hood kissed Nina, and gave her a pot of honey. But she tossed her scarlet-hooded little head at Noel as she went. Mother Hubbard passed with her dog, and she chucked Nina under the chin.

"Your cupboard shall never be bare," she said.
"And mine?" asked Noel.
"Humph," said the old lady loudly, "I don't know about you."
Dick Whittington was the only person kind to him, and even he was

The Procession of Nursery Rhymes.

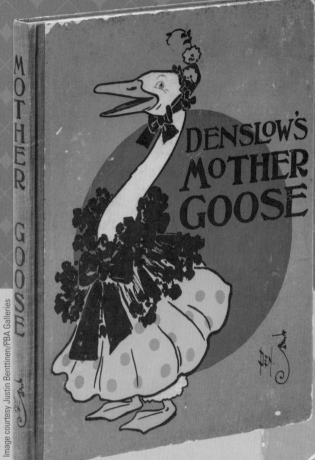

There was an old woman
who lived in a shoe,
She had so many children she
didn't know what to do;
She gave them some broth
with plenty of bread,
She kissed them all fondly
and sent them to bed.

**Denslow's Mother Goose:
Being the Old Familiar
Nursery Rhymes and Jingles**
by W.W. Denslow. McClure,
Philips & Company, New York, 1901.

Edited and illustrated by Denslow, First Edition, Second
state of Denslow's lovely traditional Mother Goose
rhymes, illustrated throughout in color. **$600** at auction.

Hey! diddle, diddle,
The cat and the fid[
The cow jumped over
the moon;
The little dog laughed
to see such sport,
And the dish ran
after the spoon.

Mother Goose

by Walter Jerrold, Blackie & Sons Limited, London, 1909.

Illustrations include frontispiece by John Hassall, noted English artist known for his poster designs and advertisements. A good auction buy at **$540**.

Image courtesy Justin Benttinen/PBA Galleries

MY FAVORITES: 1900-1919

Peter Pan by J. M. Barrie (1928):

Richly worded, darkly tragic and most certainly not politically correct. These aspects of this famous adventure tale may make modern parents shy away from reading it with your child, but I say *don't let it!* The combination of imagination, adventure, nostalgia and deeply moving musings on youth and aging will keep the whole family thinking about it long after you've put it down.

The Wind in the Willows by Kenneth Grahame, illusrated by E.H. Shepard (1908):

Patience may be needed with the pacing and language of this one, but the effort is greatly rewarded with the weird, wild adventures of the strangely civilized, anthropomorphic friends Mole, Rat, Toad and Badger. A tribute to the beauty of nature with poignant reflections on friendship, loyalty and community. You'll bring your kids to this tale and the infamous Mr. Toad will make them stay.

The Wonderful Wizard of Oz
by L. Frank Baum (1900):

Whether the movie is responsible for *Wizard's* lasting legacy or not, there's no doubt that Baum created the classic American fairytale, one that continues to be passed on from one generation to the next. Despite Baum's claim that the story is an attempt to lighten up the old style fairytales that preceded it, know that it still reflects those stories and that rewards and punishments for good and bad are numerous and quite blunt.

Anne of Green Gables
by Lucy Maud Montgomery (1908):

I've lost count of the number of times our daughter has read this book about Anne Shirley, an orphan girl with a vocabulary way beyond her age, an inordinate appreciation for the beauty of nature and the ability to get herself into — and out of — one "scrape" after the next. A timeless classic that still pleases today.

The Tale of Peter Rabbit
by Beatrix Potter (1902):

The pleasingly delicate illustrations of Potter's many children's books are familiar, comforting and essential to childhood more than 100 years later. Peter is Potter's first and most-enduring tale, told in blunt nursery-rhyme style: danger is near and there are lessons to be learned. Potter was one of the more interesting and unique women of her time outside of her remarkable children's books, making significant contributions in the disciplines of Natural Science and Conservation.

First Edition, first printing, in publisher's original binding and pictorial dust jacket. **$812.50**

Image courtesy Heritage Auctions

The Secret Garden by Frances Hodgson Burnett (1911):

This sweet story wrapped in flowery, romantic language and Yorkshire dialect remains relevant and I'll tell you why: lonely Mary and sickly Colin heal themselves and the adults around them by connecting with the magic of the English moors. They play outdoors, exercise and eat good food. Exactly what I'd say we all need today to cure our modern malaise!

Gift of the Magi by O. Henry (1906):

While technically not children's literature, I can't help but include it. *Magi* is a wonderful short story to read during whatever winter holiday your family celebrates. Its message of sacrifice and generosity remains quite relevant, and children always enjoy and think about the classic irony presented so well by such a great storyteller.

Raggedy Ann Stories by Johnny Gruelle (1918):

What is it about stories where dolls and toys have a life of their own that is so appealing to children? Here is one of the first. It's interesting to note that Gruelle created the doll before he wrote the tales. Our favorite moments in this first book of the series are when Raggedy Ann goes up on a kite and, of course, when she gets a candy heart transplant that says *I Love You*. The whole series of books include the famous Raggedy Andy, appealing to boys as well.

Just So Stories by Rudyard Kipling (1902):

Certainly Aesop's Fables and Grimm's Fairytales take the majority of the spotlight for fables of old when it comes to speculating on life and its lessons, but I really enjoyed Kipling's origin stories as a girl. Weird, wild tales about why things are the way they are (How the Camel Got His Hump, How the Rhinoceros Got His Skin) that give children a little bit of insight into the way humans struggle to make sense of our astonishing world.

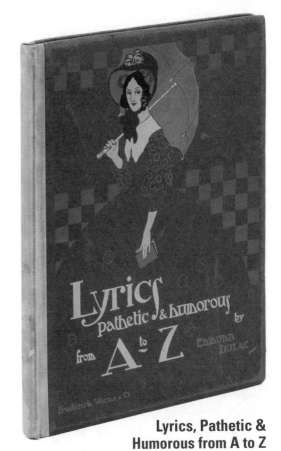

Lyrics, Pathetic & Humorous from A to Z
by Edmund Dulac,
Frederick Warne and Co., London, 1906.

Illustrated by Dulac. Hard-to-find work by the young Dulac, with amusing rhymes like "E" was an exquisite elf, "I" was an impudent imp, "L" a lorn little lass, "R" was a rubicund rustic, etc. **$204**.

Image courtesy Justin Benttinen/PBA Galleries

First Edition of this famous collection of poems, illustrated by Kipling. A good copy like this fetched **$469**.

Image courtesy Heritage Auctions

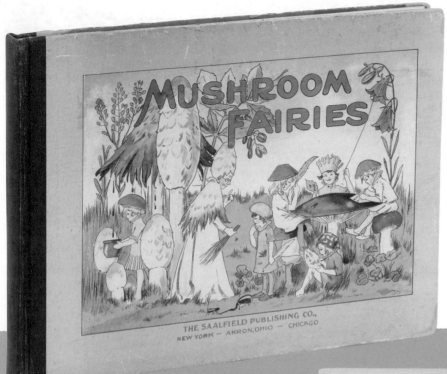

Mushroom Fairies

by Adah Louise Sutton,
Saalfield Publishing Company,
Akron, Ohio, 1910.

First Edition. A rare children's book
authored by the wife of publisher
Arthur Saalfield, best known for her
continuation of the Peter Rabbit stories
of Beatrix Potter, penned under the
name Louise A. Field. **$1,020**.

Image courtesy Justin Benttinen/PBA Galleries

Randolph Caldecott, *Come Lasses and Lads*
London: George Routledge and Sons, 1884.

First Edition. While Caldecott is not much appreciated today as
an artist in his own right, this is because his work is not well
known. One look at any of his titles, however, shows us his
obvious charm and talent as an artist. None other than Maurice
Sendak considered him the father of the modern picture book —
the top prize in picture books does carry his name, after all. This
book, in good condition, would bring about **$175**.

Image courtesy Heritage Auctions

Group of Six Picture Books

by Randolph Caldecott, bound as a single volume.

Includes *A Frog He Would A-Wooing Go*, *The Milkmaid*, *Ride a Cock-Horse to Banbury Cross* and *A Farmer Went Trotting Upon His Greymare*, *The Great Panjandrum Himself*, *Come Lasses and Lads*, and *An Elegy on the Glory of Her Sex*, *Mrs. Mary Blaize*. Published by George Routledge, ca. 1880s. In very good condition this volume went for **$200**.

Image courtesy Heritage Auctions

Rebecca of Sunnybrook Farm

by Kate Douglas Wiggin, Boston: Houghton, Mifflin, 1903.

First Edition, fourth printing. A classic book, immensely popular in its time and still read today – a magical feat for a book to hold up more than a century later. In good condition, this book will fetch about **$40**.

Image courtesy Heritage Auctions

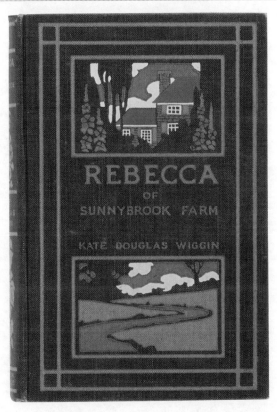

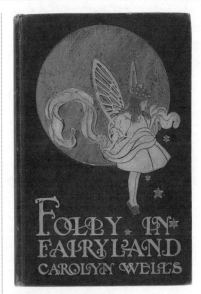

Folly in Fairyland

by Carolyn Wells, Henry Altemus, 1901.

First Edition, first printing, illustrated with 12 plates. A book that typifies the early 20th century obsession with fairies and fantasy. **$40** in an online auction.

Image courtesy Heritage Auctions

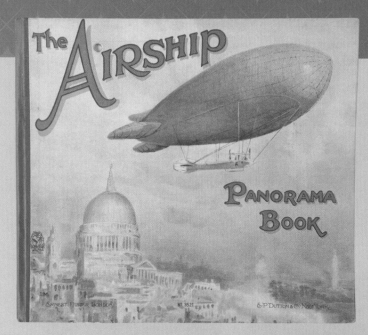

The Airship
Panorama Book

by Ernst Nister, London: Ernst Nister and New York: E. P. Dutton & Co., circa 1910.

First Edition, illustrated by Ernst Nister. Four pop-up color scenes featuring airships in various situations and accompanying text in verse. Nister's company was in Nuremberg, a center for toy making in the late 19th century and his books were very popular all over the world. Between 1891 and 1900, his company produced many children's books of superior quality in both illustration and printing. A copy like this, with all the pop-ups in working order, will bring **$600** at auction.

Image courtesy of Heritage Auctions

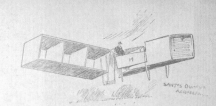

A Flight over the Harbour

O*VER* the harbour and its waters blue
    The aeroplane and its bold steerer flew;
High, high above the "lady" with the light,
That ships can see for miles and miles at night.

I rather think the birds upon the wing
Said to each other, "What a queer shaped thing!
That man who sits inside quite mad must be;
Why doesn't he grow wings like you and me?"

To be a bird—that must indeed be grand,
And skim so easily o'er sea and land,
But we to build an aeroplane are bound,
If we should wish to leave our native ground.

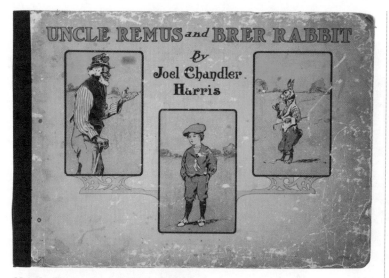

Uncle Remus and Brer Rabbit

by Joel Chandler Harris, New York: Frederick A. Stokes, 1907.

First Edition, first printing. This is a good edition that brought **$81**. This book would, of course, go on to inspire Walt Disney to make his legendary adaptation for the screen. The movie and the book were controversial at the time and remain so today. That controversy, however, cannot diminish the pop culture impact of the title.

Image courtesy Heritage Auctions

Uncle Remus Returns

by Joel Chandler Harris, Boston & New York: Houghton Mifflin, 1918.

First Edition, in rare dust jacket. **$688**

Image courtesy Heritage Auctions

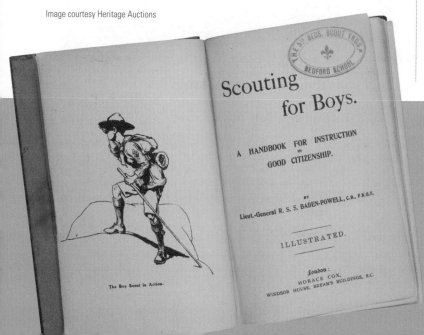

Scouting for Boys. A Handbook for Instruction in Good Citizenship

by Lieut.-General R. S. S. Baden Powell C. B., London, Horace Cox, 1908.

First Edition, first issue. A rarity in any condition, this copy brought **$10,000** at auction.

Image courtesy Heritage Auctions

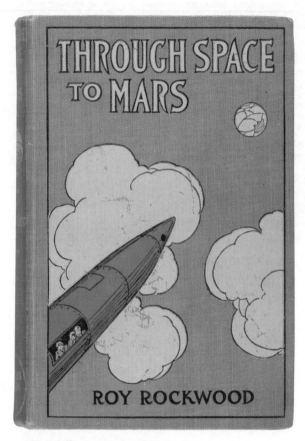

The Swiss Family Robinson

by David Wyss, Harper, 1909.

A later edition – the book was originally published in the early 1800s – in good condition, **$34** at auction. *The Swiss Family Robinson* was an incredibly popular book in its day, and through the 1970s, aided in large part by the Disney movie, which, if not totally faithful to the original story, extended the shelf life of Wyss's tale – now believed to have been created by his father – of a family stranded on a deserted island.

Image courtesy Heritage Auctions

Through Space to Mars

by Roy Rockwood, New York: Cupples & Leon, 1910.

An early 20th century book that reflects the growing awareness and public obsession with technology and space travel. Volumes like this are always fascinating in how they predicted the future and the methods of space travel more than half a century before we reached the moon. **$95** online at auction.

Image courtesy Heritage Auctions

All the Way Round
Pictures and Rhymes

Mechanical Children's Book by Maud Carlton,
London: Ernest Nister and New York:
C.P. Dutton & Co., 1899.

An enchanting children's book containing many
poems illustrated with unusual revolving pictures
that reveal hidden images beneath. **$359** at auction.

Image courtesy Heritage Auctions

W*HEN* duckies leave their farmyard pool,
  And go, just like these three,
To study at a quack-quack school,
  The art of A B C,
With the old white Drake to set them sums,
  In a college cap and gown,
Oh, you'll agree with me 'twill be
  The world turned upside down:

When bunnies leave their hutch of wood,
  And up and down the street
Go selling greenstuff fresh and good,
  For you and I to eat;
When their "Carrots fine,
  a penny a bunch,"
You hear them loudly shout,
  Oh, you'll agree with me 'twill be
  The world turned inside out!

DUCKS do sums! and bunnies keep shop!
IT makes one wonder where they'll stop!

PETER PAN

eter Pan was the brainchild of Scottish playwright J. M. Barrie. In fact, Peter Pan's first real success came as a stage play in 1904. It wasn't until 1911 that Barrie set the story of the-boy-who-never-grew-up down on the page, expanding the play and creating the beloved book that debuted as Peter and Wendy.

There's not a tremendous amount that needs to be said about the success of Peter Pan. It's wildly successful in every medium it's tackled. The book has never been out of print, the play is still performed to this day, numerous movies have been made out of it (most famously Disney's 1953 cartoon version of it, cartoons have been based on it and the merchandising side of Peter Pan is still as alive and well as it ever has been, even if it is now his sidekick, the fairy Tinker Bell, who handles most of the heavy lifting.

What we feel is sometimes overlooked, however, is the greatness of Barrie's book. This is a heartbreaking story of innocence and aging that is still poignant today. We're always deeply moved by the sensitivity and brutality of the story, as well as by Captain Hook's profound search for "good form." The salvation Hook finds, as he is falling to his death knowing that Peter showed "bad form" in tricking the captain into his demise may well be the most heartbreaking piece of it all. The truth is that Peter will move onto other adventures in a heartbeat and his entire dalliance with "Captain Codfish" will have been no more than a mere blip on his eternal boyhood radar, while for Hook is was the obsession of his life.

Peter Pan can be collected in many ways and numerous editions. With a little patience and firm idea of what you want to pay, there are many nice printings available to complement your library for a few hundred dollars or less. The most desirable of all are the first editions of Rackham-illustrated version. Expect to pay a few thousand dollars for a nice copy.

Image courtesy Heritage Auctions

The Peter Pan Portfolio
Arthur Rackham, illustrator, J. M. Barrie,
New York: Brentano's, 1914.

First Edition, American issue, number 9 of 300 limited edition copies. This fine copy brought **$2,125** at auction.

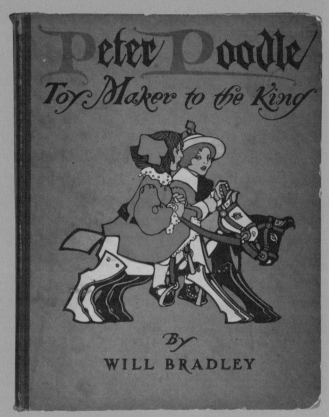

Peter Poodle Toy Maker to the King
by Will Bradley, New York:
Dodd, Mead & Company, 1906.

First Edition, illustrated throughout by the author. A sound
copy of an uncommon early 20th century work. **$100**.

Image courtesy Heritage Auctions

Poems of Childhood
by Eugene Field, Maxfield Parrish, illustrator,
New York: Scribner's, 1904.

First Edition. In fine condition, this realized **$138** online.
Parrish had an incomparable touch with color and mood: his
skills are fully on display here.

Image courtesy Heritage Auctions

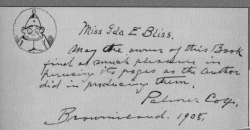

Miss Ida E Bliss.

May the owner of this Book
find as much pleasure in
perusing its pages as the author
did in producing them.

Palmer Cox,

Brownieland. 1908.

The Brownies Around The World
by Palmer Cox, Century, Co., New York,
late 1800s/early 1900s.

First Edition. The fourth book in the Brownies series.
Inscribed by Cox on the front free endpaper with a
small sketch of a Brownie. Inscription dated 1908.
$330 to a lucky collector at auction. Palmer Cox's
Brownies were incredibly popular in the early 20th
century and a major influence on American Pop
Culture at the time.

Image courtesy of Justin Benttinen/PBA Galleries

THE BROWNIES IN TURKEY.

In secret places skirmished
round
Where strangers no admittance
found
And all the household,
by decree,
Were safely under
lock and key.

They chatted freely
of the way
Some people live
at this late
day,
In spite of all that has been
done
To work reforms beneath
the sun.
86

Nine Bobbsey Twins Books

by Laura Lee Hope.

Including: *The Bobbsey Twins at Snow Lodge, The Bobbsey Twins Camping Out, The Bobbsey Twins at the County Fair, The Bobbsey Twins in Washington, The Bobbsey Twins on Blueberry Island, The Bobbsey Twins at Home, The Bobbsey Twins' Toy Shop, The Bobbsey Twins in Eskimo Island, The Bobbsey Twins Treasure Hunting*, all first editions and all published in New York: Grosset & Dunlap Publishers, various years between 1916 and 1936. This entire grouping of these very popular early 20th century books could be yours at auction in the range of **$180**.

Image courtesy Heritage Auctions

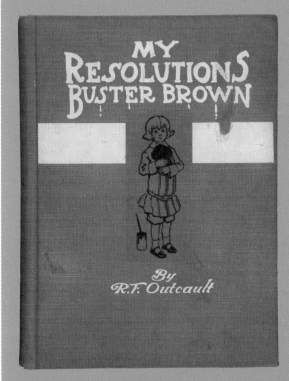

My Resolutions Buster Brown

by R. F. Outcault, Chicago:
Published by R. F. Outcault, 1910.

Inscribed and signed with an original pencil drawing on the front free endpaper. It's hard to overstate how popular Buster Brown was – hugely influential as a comic strip, then in books, films, radio, theater and even television before landing as a spokes-character for the Brown Shoe Co. His gal, Mary Jane, and his American Pit Bull Terrier, Tyge, were fixtures in the popular consciousness of early 20th century America. A volume in good condition can be had for **$155**.

Image courtesy Heritage Auctions

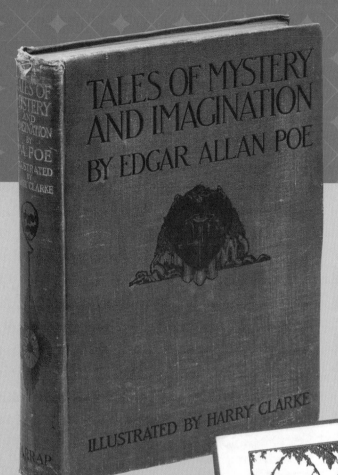

Tales of Mystery and Imagination

by Edgar Allan Poe, George G. Harrap & Co. Ltd., London, 1919.

Features 24 full-page black and white illustrations by Henry (Harry) Patrick Clarke. First Trade Edition. A high point of the illustrated books of Mr. Clarke, though the first edition, illustrated by a different artist, was published in 1908. **$30** at auction.

Image courtesy Justin Benttinen/PBA Galleries

THE TALE OF PETER RABBIT

Beatrix Potter (1866-1943) wrote more than 30 books in her life, but none had the impact and staying power of cute, mischievous little Peter Rabbit in *The Tale of Peter Rabbit.* The book has sold tens of millions of copies and been translated into dozens of languages. Peter Rabbit has also been a merchandising colossus over the decades – and there have been 11 decades of *Peter Rabbit* so far – spawning toys, games, cartoons and advertising that would make the most fervent marketers proud. Not bad for a little fur ball.

What is it that we all love about Peter Rabbit? Perhaps it's the blue coat, or Potter's amazing, expressive drawings. Perhaps it's how, after being chased through hell and creation all over Mr. McGregor's garden – and narrowly escaping certain death – his mother doses him, charmingly, with chamomile tea and simply sends him to bed.

What we love about *Peter Rabbit* is that the story was far ahead of its time. While cute, Peter Rabbit, through his own mischievousness, ends up in dire circumstances. His hubris is humbled as he runs for his life from a very palpable and capable enemy whose only goal is to destroy our hero. It's a nursery school version of *The Terminator.*

When Potter wrote *Peter Rabbit,* she initially published it herself in a small printing, after which time it was picked up by a larger publisher and the rest is children's book history. *Peter Rabbit,* and all the titles

The Tale of Peter Rabbit
by Beatrix Potter, 1902.

First edition, first printing, in publisher's original binding and pictorial dust jacket. Still a highly influential and popular book, this edition went for **$813** at auction We can remember our daughter definitely did not like the picture of poor Peter, snagged on the fence, crying his eyes out in despair as he was certain the farmer was about to capture him — never fear, though, with the help of two little birds Peter gets away.

The Tale of Squirrel Nutkin

by Beatrix Potter, London: Frederick Warne and Co., 1903.

First edition, fair condition, realized **$81** at auction.

Image courtesy Heritage Auctions

that Potter wrote (many of which are illustrated here) are infinitely collectible. There have been numerous editions and special editions and anniversary editions of the book, all with collecting cache'. All the matters, really, is your budget. For the 1902 first edition, expect to pay anywhere from several hundred dollars to close to $1,000. If you can get your hands on one of Potter's original 250 self-published editions… Well, friend, be ready to pay tens of thousands for that.

The Tale of Mrs. Tiggy-Winkle

by Beatrix Potter, Frederick Warne and Co., London, 1905.

First edition with 27 color plates by Potter and a title-page vignette. **$540** at auction.

Image courtesy Justin Benttinen/PBA Galleries.

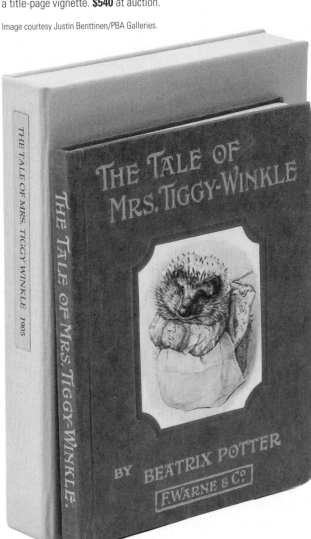

Image courtesy Justin Benttinen/PBA Galleries

Image courtesy Heritage Auctions

The Tailor of Gloucester
by Beatrix Potter, privately printed, London, 1902.

First edition, one of 500 copies. Privately printed for Potter a year before the Frederick Warne edition. The text is longer than that in the published edition and with the only appearance of the cover illustration, accounting for the steep **$4,200** price, but worth it for the rarity.

The Tailor of Gloucester
by Beatrix Potter, London: Frederick Warne & Co., Ltd, 1903.

A presentation copy, inscribed by Beatrix Potter with an autograph letter signed by her: Later printing, a presentation copy, inscribed by Potter on the front free endpaper. Inscribed copies, along with any signed copy of a Potter work, are very desirable. While this copy sold for **$7,500** to an advanced collector, it presents a good lesson to beginners, in that this title comes from deeper in the Potter canon. Good collectors will start with the less sought-after titles of their favorite author and build up to the big ones. Patience is a virtue – something that Peter Rabbit sorely needed to learn! An unsigned, uninscribed early printing of this same book might be had for just **$100-$200**.

There are few books that can claim the cultural influence of L. Frank Baum's *The Wonderful Wizard of Oz*. From its first printing, in spring of 1900, the book and the world it introduced, *Oz*, have been wildly popular, across generations and, now, across centuries. What Baum sought with his stories, and what he got, was a complete shift in the children's storytelling

The Wonderful Wizard of Oz

by L. Frank Baum, Chicago and New York: George M. Hill Company, 1900

First edition. Overall, a very good copy, much better and brighter than is usually seen, the first and best-known of Baum's Oz series and immortalized by the 1939 MGM movie starring Judy Garland. No surprise then that it brought **$9,375** at auction.

Image courtesy Heritage Auctions

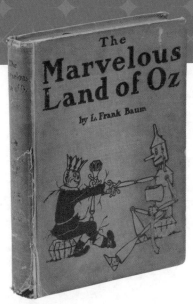

The Marvelous Land of Oz

by L. Frank Baum, Reilly & Britton, Chicago, 1904

In good condition, this copy brought **$180** at auction.

Image courtesy Justin Benttinen/PBA Galleries

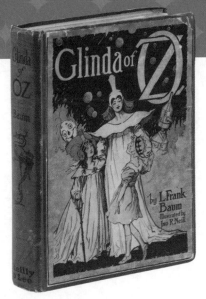

Glinda of Oz

by L. Frank Baum, Reilly & Lee, Chicago, 1929

First edition, first printing. **$120** at auction.

Image courtesy Justin Benttinen/PBA Galleries

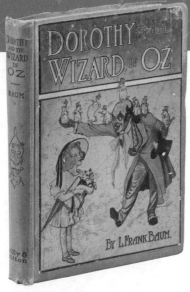

Dorothy and the Wizard of Oz

by L. Frank Baum, The Reilly & Britton Co., Chicago, 1908

First state printing. A good price at **$168**.

Image courtesy Justin Benttinen/PBA Galleries

landscape of the turn of the 20th century.

Most of the modern world knows *The Wonderful Wizard of Oz* as the film *The Wizard of Oz*, arguably the most famous and influential film of all time, but the story of Dorothy Gale and her little dog Toto swept away by a tornado to Oz and the Wicked Witch she must fight to get home largely sprang from this, the first *Oz* book.

Baum would write 14 *Oz* books total, a good share of the more than 50 books he wrote in his career, and he would be widely venerated in his time, seeing fabulous success and amassing serious wealth in the process.

He died in 1919, at the age of 63. One can only wonder what he would have thought of the film version of his work and of its enduring success and influence.

All of the *Oz* books are relatively easy to find if you're looking to collect. First editions of *The Wonderful Wizard of Oz,* in good condition, will bring several thousand dollars – well more than $5,000 and up to $10,000 – and first editions of the following books can be had in the range of $100, give or take a few dollars depending on condition. Entire sets of later editions can still be found, are entirely affordable and still make great reading.

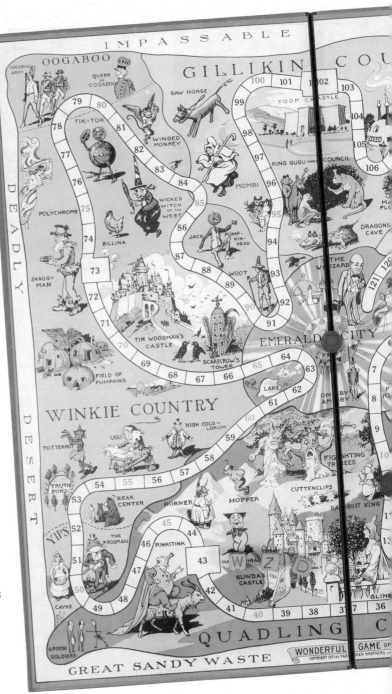

THE WONDERFUL GAME OF OZ

Board game based on the books by L. Frank Baum, Parker Brothers, Salem, Mass., ca. 1922

Folding color pictorial game board, eight page rule booklet, three wooden dice each spelling the word W-I-Z-A-R-D, four turned wood playing pieces with original two-part box and full-size color pictorial label on top. According to Greene & Martin in The Oz Scrapbook (p. 174), "In 1921 Parker Brothers issued The Wonderful Game of Oz, a Parcheesi-like game whose folding playing board was a large map of Oz, beautifully lithographed in colors, with all the Oz characters shown in their proper locations..." The characters moved along the Yellow Brick Road according to their throws. A rarity, for sure, this game brought **$480** at auction.

Image courtesy Justin Benttinen/PBA Galleries

Tik-Tok of Oz
by L. Frank Baum,
Reilly & Britton, Chicago, 1914
First edition, first printing. **$120**.

Image courtesy of Justin Benttinen/ PBA Galleries.

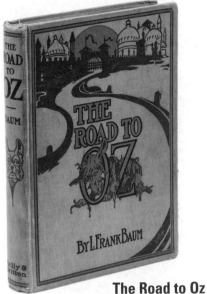

The Road to Oz
by L. Frank Baum,
Reilly & Britton, Chicago, 1909
First edition, first printing. **$120+** at auction.

Image courtesy Justin Benttinen/
PBA Galleries.

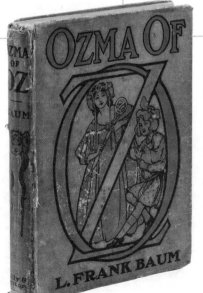

Ozma of Oz
by L. Frank Baum, Reilly &
Britton, Chicago, 1907

First edition, first printing.
Expect to pay about **$120+** for
this book, in good condition, at
a reputable dealer or auction
house.

Image courtesy Justin Benttinen/
PBA Galleries

LEWIS CARROLL

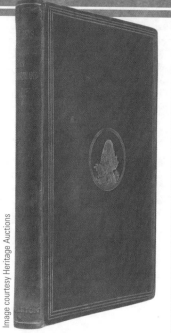

Alice's Adventures in Wonderland

by Lewis Carroll, New York: D. Appleton and Co., 1866.

First American Edition (i.e., First Edition, second issue), with 42 wood engravings and a wood-engraved frontispiece after illustrations by John Tenniel. This copy realized **$5,975**, a healthy price for a great copy of this transcendent, whimsical and terrifying tale.

Okay, so *Alice in Wonderland* was written by Lewis Carroll (born Charles Lutwidge Dodgson) in 1865, some 35 years before the arbitrary beginning time period for this book. The simple truth is, however, that *Alice* is that rare book that speaks individually to each generation that encounters it, speaks its wonderful nonsense to all age of readers and has never been out of print. That's 150 years. If ever a book has earned the "timeless" designation, then it is this one.

Every children's book written since Lewis Carroll set *Alice* down on paper owes this particular book a tremendous debt of gratitude. While generally classified as "nonsense," in the strictest sense of term, its sensibilities predate a whole host of artistic movements (Modernism, Absurdism, Surrealism, Postmodernism, to name a few) that would take concepts of logic and argument directly from *Alice*. Children's books may have most directly benefited, but it is just a single artistic niche to do so.

It's interesting to note that *Alice in Wonderland* did not meet with much critical praise when it was released in England in 1865. While it sold well from the beginning, it would be a few decades before critics and scholars elevated to the lofty perch that it now occupies.

There are so many different editions and artists that have tackled *Alice* that the full accounting would likely fill a whole other book. If you're looking for collectible *Alice* books, always go for the first edition, whether it's the true first edition (American or English), which can run several thousand dollars, or the first edition of a later printing, with price depending on the edition and the artist.

Alice's Adventures in Wonderland

by Lewis Carroll, illustrated by Will Pogany, E.P. Dutton, New York, 1929

First edition of this volume with illustrations by Willy Pogany, one of the most popular children's illustrators of the early 20th century. Alice has never been out of print and this edition just goes to show that illustrators have always been fascinated by the material and continue to be so through today. This volume, with the rare dust jacket, brought **$1,080** at auction.

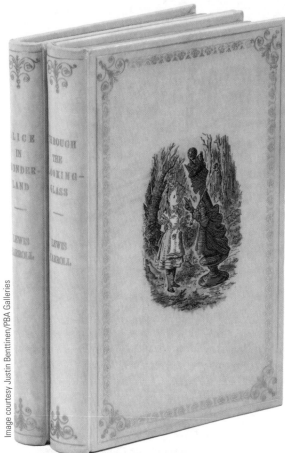

IN A LITTLE BILL.   55

Hardly knowing what she did, she picked up
a little bit of stick, and held it out to the
puppy; whereupon the puppy jumped into the
air off all its feet at once, with a yelp of

A MAD TEA-PARTY.   97

The Hatter opened his eyes very wide on
hearing this; but all he *said* was, "Why is a
raven like a writing-desk?"

"Come, we shall have some fun now!"
thought Alice. "I'm glad they've begun asking riddles — I believe I can guess that," she
added aloud.

"Do you mean that you think you can find
out the answer to it?" said the March Hare.

"Exactly so," said Alice.

Alice's Adventures in Wonderland, and Through the Looking-Glass and What Alice Found There

by Lewis Carroll, Lee and Shepard, Boston, 1869 and 1872

Two later printings of the original and its les popular sequel,
with the original illustrations by John Tenniel. These are the first
editions to be printed in America. They realized **$3,300** at auction.

Chapter 2

BETWEEN THE WARS

(1920-1939)

Out of the schism of war at the end of the second decade of the 20th century would emerge some of the greatest children's books, and creators, the world would ever see. Many of these writers and artists created work that remains quite important today.

The world, out of necessity after World War I, grew up. Economies recovered, soldiers re-entered society and life in the Western Hemisphere, for the most part, settled into a sense of normalcy. Soon enough, led by advances in film, radio and printing, the appetite for children's literature returned. It proved to be an extremely rich period, led by writers and artists who were looking back at their own childhoods through the veil of war and privation. The innocence of childhood was suddenly no longer just for the children living it, it was for the adults who had grown up and lost it.

The hunger of nostalgia as we know it was born. The writers of the first 20 years of the 1900s were not necessarily nostalgic for their lost youth, or at least it did not show in much of their work. Childhood was presented as fluid and of the moment. After the First World War, it was not so. A mother or father reading a great book of the period to or with their children could not only open a new world to their son or daughter, they could clearly see their own experiences – both as a child and as an adult – in the tales that were being spun and the images being drawn by the very best of the day.

Another important thing began to shape the books aimed at children: marketing. It was suddenly possible, as film began to mature and cartoons provided a happily captive kid audience to marketers, to tie product in with what kids (and adults) were flocking to see in theaters on Saturdays and Sundays. The result was electrifying to the business and suddenly, with the help of Pop Culture juggernauts like Popeye the Sailor, Buck Rogers and Felix the Cat, among the many, books could be directly sold to kids cross-promoting these same characters.

Then into the fray stepped Walt Disney and the world

would never be the same. Rather than try and cover the Disney contribution here, however, the creations of the Mouse are covered in Chapter 6 of this book. If you just can't wait, skip ahead now. We'll wait for you right here.

The period of 1920-1939, arguably, belonged to a handful of characters: Winnie the Pooh, Raggedy Ann and Andy, Mary Poppins and Babar the Elephant. There were certainly hundreds of great books and characters, many of which – as you'll see in the following pages – are still enjoyed today. It is in the creations of A.A. Milne, Johnny Gruelle, P.L. Travers and Jean de Brunhoff, however, that we can trace the intense creativity of the period.

Milne's *Winnie-the-Pooh* world is perfectly encapsulated, a gentle refuge from the destruction of the preceding years. Gruelle's absurd, nonsensical *Raggedy Ann and Andy* adventures are wild and woolly, but any threatening danger is easily diffused. P.L. Travers *Mary Poppins* is compassionate and cold, ready to teach a hard lesson or provide a mystical experience, precisely what World War I had done in opening the eyes of its participants. De Brunhoff's *Babar* shows a little elephant founding an empire and civilizing a world, in essence finding his humanity. All of them are not without the influence of Eastern mysticism, an impulse perhaps initially inspired by that very sense of "now" in those authors' own childhoods in the late 1800s/early 1900s.

In this second segment of the 20th century we can see a desire for the peace of the past, for the calm of a world not rocked by the loss of innocence, yet all of them carry a certain sense of foreboding – perhaps it is the onset of adulthood or perhaps it was the march of totalitarianism that began in the early 1930s. No matter what, this era, too, would come to a screeching halt as war consumed Europe. Children's books continued publication in America, but it was only with a wary eye on what was happening across the pond. War was coming and profound change was once again in the wind.

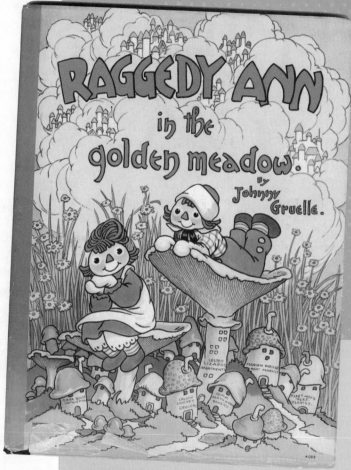

Raggedy Ann in the Golden Meadow
By Johnny Gruelle, Hardcover Children's Book File Copy, Whitman, 1935: **$79**.

Image courtesy Heritage Auctions

Millions of Cats
by Wanda Ga'g, Coward McCann, New York, 1928.

No. 184 of 250 copies, First Edition with an original signed woodcut by Ga'g laid in, as issued. Signed by the author/ illustrator at the limitation statement. A high spot of 20th century children's literature, this book won a Newbery Honor award in 1929, a rare occurrence for a picture book. *Millions of Cats* has remained in print since its initial publication, the oldest American picture book that can claim this. This special copy brought **$7,200**.

Image courtesy Justin Benttinen/PBA Galleries

MILLIONS OF CATS

Once upon a time there was a very old man and a very old woman. They lived in a nice clean house which had flowers all around it, except where the door was. But they couldn't be happy because they were so very lonely.

Histoire de Babar: Le Petit Elephant

by Jean de Brunhoff.
Jardin des Modes, Paris, 1931.

Illustrated in color throughout. First Edition of the first book in the series about Babar and his elephant kingdom. **$1,200** at auction.

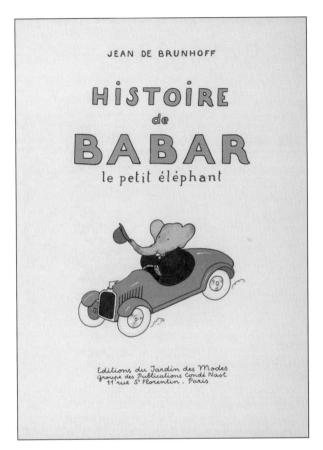

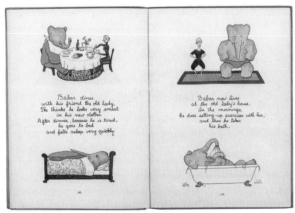

MY FAVORITES: 1920-1939

The Story of Doctor Dolittle
by Hugh Lofting (1920):

One of the great characters of children's literature, Dr. Dolittle is also a favorite in our family. As with many books from the early 1900s, the depictions of the non-Anglo characters are astonishingly insensitive and will need to be explained by parents — editions edited for the "modern audience" can help with this dilemma. Bottom line: don't miss out on the adventures of this kind and generous veterinarian who can speak the languages of all animals and much prefers their company to that of humans.

Caddie Woodlawn
by Carol Ryrie Brink (1935):

Not only is *Caddie Woodlawn* an invaluable piece of history told through the eyes of Brink's grandmother via stories from her youth spent as a pioneer during the 1860s in Wisconsin (overshadowed by the better-known Little House books), it's also thoroughly enjoyable and accessible almost a century later. I can't help but feel jealous of the long hours the children spend outside in such unspoiled nature. Children will be fascinated by how the settlers lived then — how they prepared food, how they got news, how they depended upon each other. The spunky, brave-hearted Caddie will win them over as she works hard to become a "lady."

Mary Poppins by P.L. Travers (1934):

We read this book to our daughter before we showed her the movie, a pattern that has been repeated across numerous great books that were turned into good movies. Having not read this book when we were young, we were simply astounded at the depth of this quirky tale filled with Eastern mysticism and Greek mythology. Cranky, impatient, omniscient — maybe immortal — Mary Poppins is perhaps the most unique and interesting character of children's literature.

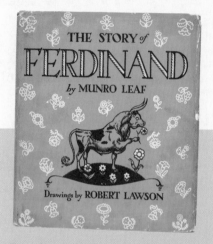

The Story of Ferdinand by Munro Leaf, illustrated by Robert Lawson (1936):

The beautiful and timeless story of a bull who would prefer to sniff flowers than fight. Although the author denied any political agenda, it drew much controversy upon its publication. The simple but important message of being yourself is always relevant and can be used to discuss a range of topics with children, from bullying to non-violence, to stereotypes and beyond.

Ben and Me by Robert Lawson (1939):

My husband and I wondered how well this tale, which we fondly remembered, would hold up when we read it with our daughter. For the most part, it holds up quite well. Perhaps it's a bit dated, and the language can be difficult for youngsters, but this tale of the mouse that lived with Ben Franklin (and did most of the work) is a real hoot.

Mr. Popper's Penguins
by Richard and Florence Atwater (1938):

This was always one of my favorites as a child. What an absurdly pleasing tale about a housepainter and his family who end up hosting a family of penguins in their home and then taking the act on the road. The language is dated, yes, and the story takes odd twists and turns, but it does indeed hold up.

Henner's Lydia by Marguerite de Angeli (1936):

A family favorite passed down to my father from his family and from my father to me. This beautifully illustrated story follows a few days in the life of Lydia, an Amish girl living in Lancaster County, PA. One of the first works written by this highly honored author, it's based on the real lives of the Amish community, well-researched and fully-fleshed out. A fantastic piece of historical fiction for children, you get an appreciation for the beauty and simplicity of the life, along with an appreciation for the hard work and strict rules that governed their lives. Since the communities still exist today, it's worth a road trip after reading.

Little Tim and the Brave Sea Captain
by Edward Ardizzone (1936):

This lively tale of a boy who dreams of being a sailor remains enchanting, largely due to Ardizzone's incredible watercolor and pen and ink illustrations. The story is dated, which gives it a charm, but also necessitates parental guidance around topics like talking to strangers, getting parent's permission and danger.

Mike Mulligan and His Steam Shovel
by Virginia Lee Burton (1939):

In this age of modern technology, it feels so good to root for Mary Anne, the old-fashioned steam powered machine, as she and Mike endeavor to dig the town cellar in just one day with the whole community watching. With such simple and pleasing illustrations, and a satisfying ending, too, this book is fun for children and bittersweet nostalgia for adults.

Velveteen Rabbit by Margery Williams (1922):

What's not to love about this sentimental classic about a toy bunny's quest to become real? What child hasn't thought at some point that their stuffed animal is secretly alive? Williams is a skilled storyteller and knows just how to tug at the heartstrings. An endlessly discussable book. Meryl Streep's audio version of the book is well worth seeking out.

The Story About Ping
by Marjorie Flack (1933):

This book is both dated and mildly irritating to our modern sensibilities in so many ways, yet it still remains one of our perennial favorites. Perhaps it is the lush, exotic illustrations, or Ping's spirited personality, or better yet the fact that he spends the entire adventure trying to avoid a spank on the bottom, which is exactly what awaits him on the last page.

Willy Pogany's Mother Goose

by Will Pogany, New York: Thomas Nelson and Sons, 1928.

First Edition. **$325** at auction.

Image courtesy Heritage Auctions

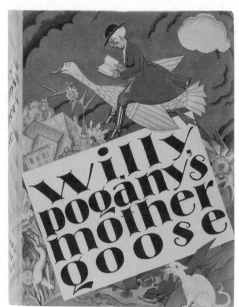

The Sleeping Beauty

by C.S. Evans, Arthur Rackham, illustrator, London: Heinemann, 1920.

First trade edition. **$114**.

Image courtesy Heritage Auctions

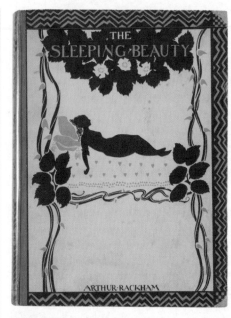

Anne of Green Gables

by L.M. Montgomery, The Page Co., Boston, 1923.

Illustrated with 24 full page plates from photographs from the 1919 silent film adaptation directed by William Desmond Taylor and starring Mary Miles Minter as Anne, now considered a lost film. The *Anne of Green Gables* books are still very readable and engaging. **$480** at auction.

Image courtesy of Justin Benttinen/ PBA Galleries

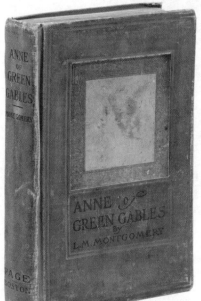

The Ship That Sailed to Mars

by William M. Timlin, London: George G. Harrap & Company Limited, 1923.

Considered one of the most original and beautiful Children's Books of the 1920s. **$3,000** at auction.

Image courtesy Heritage Auctions

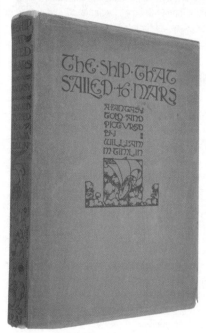

By the time Ping was right side up his mother and his father and his aunts were already marching, one by one, up over the bridge. By the time Ping neared the shore, his uncles and his cousins were marching over, and by the time Ping reached the shore the last of his forty-two cousins had crossed the bridge!

Ping knew he would be the last, the very last duck if he crossed the bridge. Ping did not want to be spanked.

The Story About Ping

by Marjorie Flack, Viking Press, New York. Illustrations by Kurt Wiese, 1933.

First Edition. The tale of a domesticated duck lost on the Yangtze River is still charming and still brings a laugh when Ping gets swatted on the butt for being the last duck on the boat. This lovely copy brought **$780** at auction.

Image courtesy Justin Benttinen/PBA Galleries

MARY POPPINS

Mary Poppins
by P.L. Travers, illustrated by Mary Shepard,
New York: Reynal & Hitchcock, 1934

First American edition of the author's first book (published the same year as the first English edition). **$239** at auction.

Image courtesy Heritage Auctions

Would P. L. Travers' inscrutable, mystic nanny *Mary Poppins* have had the life it's had, and the influence, were it not for Walt Disney's timeless 1964 film version of the character (based on the first four *Mary Poppins* books)?

Likely not, but for those who love the film – and count our house among them – the original *Mary Poppins* books, if you have not read them, are tremendously inspired and deeply mysterious, with Mary herself proving even more magical and enigmatic than even Julie Andrews' amazing embodiment of the character in the iconic film.

Viewed correctly, the stories of *Mary Poppins* are not only delightful childhood reads, but also a primer on Eastern Philosophy and Mythological Archetypes, with the main character embodying and encountering them all in some form or another as witnessed by the Banks children. Within these adventures you'll find several that match aspects of the film, and many that complement the 2004 Broadway musical version of the books, but even more, you'll find deeper ideas of life, love and philosophy, making the books timeless and relevant.

The 2013 Disney movie, "Saving Mr. Banks," detailed (and fictionalized) the difficult relationship between Travers, Disney and the process of creating a film version of it, and in turn shed some new light on the classic. It did not, however, do justice to Travers as a thinker. Evident in the work is her obvious worldliness and experience – she traveled the world, acted on the London stage, met W.B. Yeats, immersed herself in mythology and was deeply influenced by the teachings of George Gurdjieff – which influenced all aspects of her stories and her life.

Al White (American 20th Century), Walt Disney's Mary Poppins, Little Golden Book cover illustration, 1964

Gouache on board with an acetate and acrylic paint overlay, 16 x 13. Not signed. **$567** at auction.

Image courtesy Heritage Auctions

Mary Poppins
New York: Harcourt, Brace & Co., c.1958

Mary Poppins Comes Back
New York: Harcourt, Brace & World, c.1966

Mary Poppins Opens the Door
First American Edition, Reynal & Hitchcock, 1943

Mary Poppins in the Park,
First American Edition, New York: Harcourt, Brace & Co., 1952

Together, four volumes, all Illustrated by Mary Shepard. The first four of eight volumes in the Mary Poppins series. **$450**.

Image courtesy Justin Benttinen/PBA Galleries.

Mary Poppins Publicity Shot

Audiences joined Julie Andrews and Dick Van Dyke (center) in giving the movie *Mary Poppins* a big thumbs up. A charming and inexpensive collectible, this publicity shot from the movie sold for **$26.**

Image courtesy
Heritage Auctions

Mary Poppins (Buena Viesta, 1964) One Sheet

This very fine move poster from the Disney hit sold for **$200** at auction.

Image courtesy
Heritage Auctions

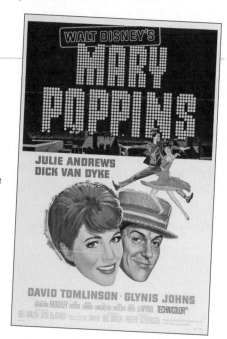

Mary Poppins (Buena Vista, 1964) Lobby Card Set of 9

Wonderful, lightly used set of lobby cards from the landmark movie starring Julie Andrews and Dick Van Dyke. A set like this, in near mint condition, brought **$388** at auction.

Image courtesy Heritage Auctions

The Story of Ferdinand

by Munro Leaf, The Viking Press,
New York, 1936.

First Edition. Ferdinand quickly became popular, striking
an anti-war chord in a world infected by turmoil. It
was reprinted multiple
times and made into an
animated film by Disney
in 1938. Amazingly,
and perhaps sadly, this
magnificent little tale is
every bit as relevant today
as it was almost 80 years
ago. For a pristine copy
like this, expect to pay in
the range of **$5,700**.

Image courtesy Justin Benttinen/
PBA Galleries

The Story of
FERDINAND

By Munro Leaf
Illustrated by Robert Lawson

THE VIKING PRESS · PUBLISHERS
New York Mcmxxxvi

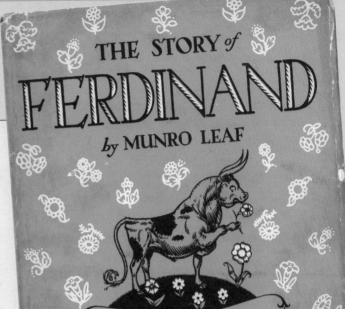

The Pirate Twins

by William Nicholson, London: Faber & Faber, 1928.

The copy pictured here is No. 46 from a "Special Signed Edition 60 Copies Only," signed by the author at the limitation statement inside the front cover. **$2,280** at auction.

Image courtesy Justin Benttinen/PBA Galleries

The Night Before Christmas

by Clement C. Moore, illustrated by Arthur Rackham, Harrap, London, 1931.

Illustrated by Arthur Rackham including four color plates. First Rackham Trade Edition. What can you really say about this beloved holiday poem? A classic that never grows old. **$390** at auction.

Image courtesy of Justin Benttinen/PBA Galleries.

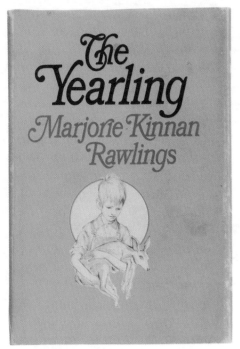

The Yearling
by Marjorie Kinnan Rawlings, New York: Scribner's, 1938.

A First Edition of this perennial classic, always popular with collectors and a story that never fails to move readers. There are still many good copies floating around at good prices. This one, which brought **$24** at auction, is the perfect book to go into a beginning collection.

Image courtesy
Heritage Auctions

Popeye with the Hag of the Seven Seas
by E. C. Segar, Pleasure Books, Inc., Chicago, 1935.

Illustrated throughout, with three-color pop-ups. **$100**.

Image courtesy Justin Benttinen/PBA Galleries

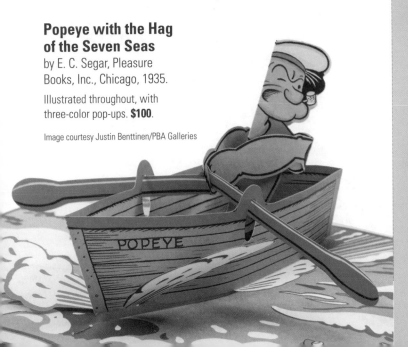

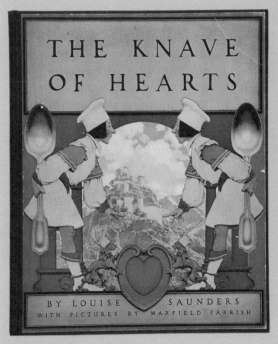

The Knave of Hearts
by Louise Sanders, Maxfield Parrish, illustrator, New York: Charles Scribner's Sons, 1925.

First Edition. A very good copy. Parrish worked for three years on the 26 remarkable paintings for the *Knave of Hearts*, even building an elaborate castle model in his workroom as a model for the artwork. This beautiful copy brought **$896** at auction, a good price for such a famous book.

Image courtesy
Heritage Auctions

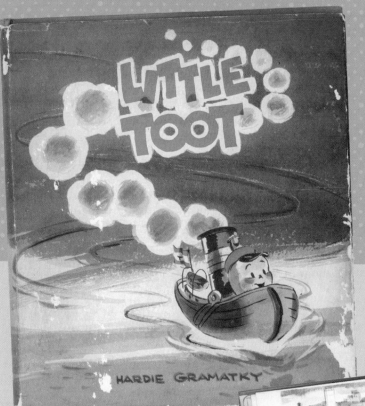

Little Toot

by Hardie Gramatky, New York:
G. P. Putnam's Sons, 1939.

First Edition of the famous story about Little Toot,
a tugboat "child," who would rather play around
than work. Inscribed by previous owner on half title:
"Edward King- His Book. Christmas 1939." **$780**.

Image courtesy Justin Benttinen/PBA Galleries

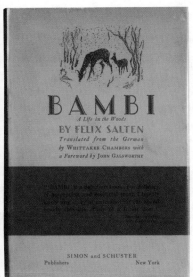

Bambi. A Life in the Woods

by Felix Salten, New York:
Simon and Schuster, 1928.

First American Edition, first printing and the first English-language edition, realized **$1,625**. This is the story of a young deer that Walt Disney immortalized in his famous cartoon *Bambi*, which is widely beloved and revered so many decades after its inception. Amazingly, *Bambi* was not too well received as a film when it came out, as critics were looking for a movie that would make a cultural impact as deep as *Snow White* did – a tall order at the time!

Image courtesy Heritage Auctions

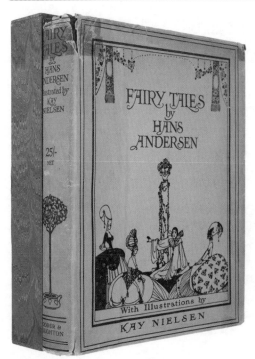

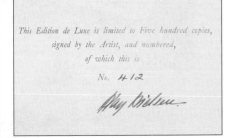

Fairy Tales

by Hans Andersen, Kay Nielsen, illustrator, London: Hodder & Stoughton, 1924.

First limited edition, one of 500 numbered copies signed by Nielsen. **$2,250**.

Image courtesy Heritage Auctions

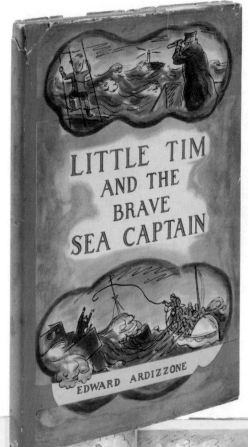

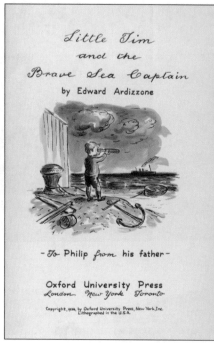

Little Tim and the Brave Sea Captain

by Edward Ardizzone. Oxford University Press, London, New York, Toronto, 1936.

First Edition, illustrated throughout by the author. Ardizzone's first and most famous book for children. Sold for **$540**.

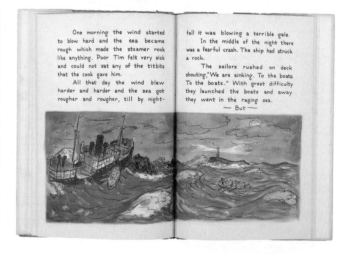

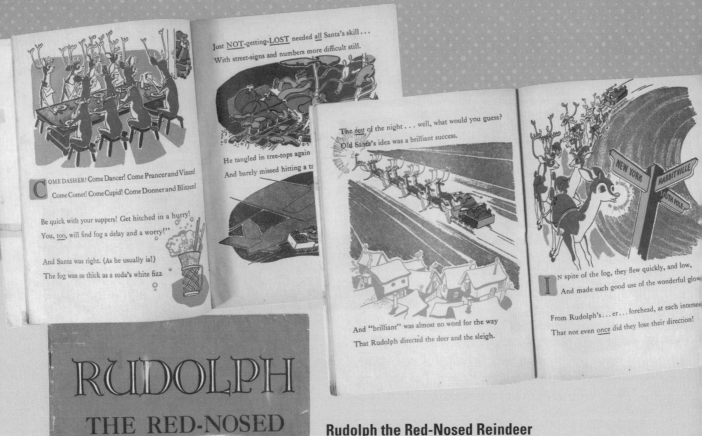

Rudolph the Red-Nosed Reindeer
by Robert L. May, Montgomery Ward.
Illustrated in color by Denver Gillen, 1939.

First Edition, first issue. In 1939, Robert L. May, at the request of his employer, Montgomery Ward & Co., wrote the story of Rudolph. May's daughter chose the name for the shiny-nosed hero of the poem. Illustrated by Denver Gillen, the book was distributed as a keepsake to the children customers of Montgomery Ward. Several years later Johnny Marks wrote lyrics based on the poem and Gene Autry recorded the song, which was to become the second best-selling record of all time. The rest is history, as they say. A First Edition like this will cost you **$600+**, a good deal in our opinion.

Image courtesy Justin Benttinen/PBA Galleries

MADELINE

What is there not to love about Ludwig Bemelmans' *Madeline*? First published in 1939, and followed by five more before the author's death in 1961 (a seventh book was found posthumously published), the books concern the spunky, fearless little redhead, Madeline, the girls she lives with in a boarding school in Paris, and the beleaguered nun that has to wrangle them all. Top to bottom, first line to last, *Madeline* is an absolute charmer.

What is perhaps the most obvious sign of the greatness of Bemelmans' heroine? The opening line and the last line of the book are absolute classics, and ones that many of us always remember: "In an old house in Paris/That was covered in vines/lived two little girls in two straight lines…" so begins the tale and "That's all there is; there isn't anymore" is how it ends. If you've read them, you remember them.

The story and art of *Madeline* make it the best of the books, though the others are massively entertaining as well, as well as the simplest. Miss Clavel, the girls' minder, wakes in the night with a feeling that something is wrong. It turns out Madeline, with a pain in her side, has to have her appendix out. She gets to go to the hospital in an ambulance, gets to stay in a bed with a crank on it and, best of all, *she has a scar on her belly* – the power of the scar to the other girls is massive. Once Madeline comes home, Miss Clavel wakes in the middle of the night once again, rushes to see her girls and finds them all crying – not because they are in pain, but because they, too, want to have their appendixes out. Brilliant and funny, what more can you ask?

You'll pay more than $1,000 for a First Edition *Madeline*, maybe $2,000. The rest will run you $100 to $250. Later editions are equally appealing and less expensive, so budget accordingly.

Madeline

by Ludwig Bemelmans, Simon and Schuster, New York, 1939.

First Edition of Bemelmans' classic children's tale. A 1940 Caldecott Medal Honors title, this edition, in good condition brought a premium price of **$1,800** at auction.

Madeline's Christmas

by Ludwig Bemelmans, 1985. Viking Kestrel, New York. Illustrated by the author.

First Edition in book form. Originally published as a special book insert in the 1956 Christmas issue of McCall's magazine. Madeline inherits a fortune from a rich uncle in Texas – Dallas, to be exact – and has quite an adventure in the famous *Neiman-Marcus* department store. **$168** at auction.

Image courtesy of Justin Benttinen/PBA Galleries

Madeline and the Bad Hat

by Ludwig Bemelmans, Viking Press, New York, 1957.

First trade edition with illustrations by the author. The third title in Bemelmans' series of Madeline tale, this copy realized **$228** at auction.

Image courtesy Justin Benttinen/PBA Galleries

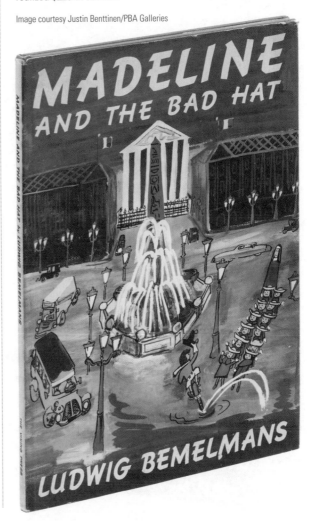

Madeline's Rescue

by Ludwig Bemelmans, Viking, New York, 1953.

First Edition and the recipient of the 1954 Caldecott Medal. A good auction buy at **$420**.

Image courtesy Justin Benttinen/ PBA Galleries

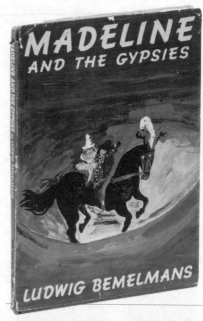

Madeline and The Gypsies

by Ludwig Bemelmans, Viking, New York, 1959.

First Edition, illustrations by the author. The fourth title in Bemelmans' wonderful Madeline series. This copy brought **$120**.

Image courtesy Justin Benttinen/PBA Galleries

Madeline in London

by Ludwig Bemelmans, Viking, New York, 1961.

The fifth title in Bemelmans' Madeline tales. **$180**.

Image courtesy of PBA Galleries

Howard Pyle's Book of Pirates

by Howard Pyle, New York: Harper & Brothers, 1921.

Compiled with a Foreword by Merle Johnson, with 38 plates (14 in color), plus several wood engravings and drawings throughout by Pyle. From an edition of 50 copies printed on vellum stock, the first printing from new plates. Quite rare is an understatement. **$510** at auction.

Image courtesy Justin Benttinen/ PBA Galleries

RAGGEDY ANN AND ANDY

Incredibly popular in their day, the *Raggedy Ann and Andy* books sprang from the personal tragedy of author Johnny Gruelle, whose daughter, Marcella, died when she was 13. To deal with his grief, Gruelle created Raggedy Ann, based on a faceless rag doll he had given his daughter, which she loved immensely. In all, more than 40 *Raggedy Ann and Andy* books were published – not all of which were written by Gruelle – and they were nothing short of a cultural phenomenon, remaining very popular through the 1970s. If their star has diminished somewhat in the last 30+ years, they are still relatively popular nonetheless. The adventures of Raggedy Ann and Andy are charming, sweet and totally surreal.

Raggedy Andy Stories
by Johnny Gruelle, P.F. Volland, Joliet, Ill, 1920.

Illustrations throughout by the author. First Edition. **$300+**

Images courtesy Justin Benttinen/PBA Galleries

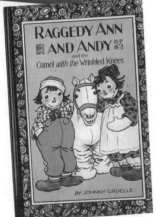

Raggedy Ann and Andy and the Camel with the Wrinkled Knees

by Johnny Gruelle, Joliet: P. F. Volland Company, 1924.

Illustrated by the author. A near fine copy, not often encountered still in the box, this will run in the range of **$700**.

Image courtesy Heritage Auctions

Raggedy Ann in Cookie Land

Illustration Original Art by M. A. Donahue, 1931.

A delightful ink with watercolor illustration of Raggedy Ann and Andy from Gruelle's children's book. They don't show up for sale too terribly often, but when they do — depending on the characters represented — expect to pay in the **$2,000** range.

Image courtesy Heritage Auctions

Three Raggedy Ann Books in Original Boxes

by Johnny Gruelle

Including: *The Paper Dragon. A Raggedy Ann Adventure*, Joliet: P. F. Volland, 1926; *Raggedy Ann's Magical Wishes*, Joliet: P. F. Volland, 1928 and *Raggedy Ann's Lucky Pennies*, Joliet: P. F. Volland, 1932. A nice trio, all in boxes, that went to a collector at auction for **$777**.

Image courtesy Heritage Auctions

A. A. MILNE

A.A. Milne's Winnie-the-Pooh may well be the most universally loved character in all of children's books. There are few characters, and few stories, that reflect such tenderness and gentleness in reflecting on the magic possibilities of childhood and fewer stories still that reflect an author's deep and abiding love for his intended audience: in

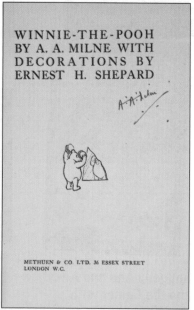

First Edition set of the four Pooh books
by A.A. Milne, each signed by the author.

This set, in their original dust jackets, brought **$23,900** at auction. Pretty steep, but worth it considering what these books represent. All of the Pooh books are magical, no matter what age you are when you read them.

this case, his son Christopher Robin. It is that love of the telling of the story and for the recipient of the story that we all identify with and which rings true every time we read these books.

The five volumes that make of all the Winnie The Pooh books – *When We Were Very Young; Winnie-the-Pooh; Now We Are Six; The House at Pooh Corner; The Christopher Robin Story Book* – are well known to most people in the Western Hemisphere. They are the various adventures of Christopher Robin and best friend and stuffed Teddy Bear, Pooh. Along for the various rides are all of Pooh's friends: Piglet, Owl, Tigger, Kanga and Roo, Eeyore, Rabbit and all of Rabbit's relations.

The characters are timeless and the lessons of the story gentle, funny and easily relatable. They are also infused with all kinds of allegory and parable, easily integrated into one's worldview, whatever it may be. Each one of us can see ourselves in any one of the characters of the books – quick, which *Pooh* character would *you* be? – and we can all identify with dilemmas and fears that face them throughout the books.

More than 20 million copies of *Winnie The Pooh* have been sold, so they are easy to find in almost any bookstore or online sale or auction. First Editions are highly coveted and will cost you several thousand dollars, especially if Milne signed or inscribed them. The good news is that you don't need a First Edition to enjoy the *Pooh* stories repeatedly. Any copy will do for that.

A. A. Milne, first American Editions of all of the Pooh Books and *The Christopher Robin Story Book*
New York: E. P. Dutton & Co., Inc., 1924-1929.

Titles include: *When We Were Very Young; Winnie-the-Pooh; Now We Are Six; The House at Pooh Corner; The Christopher Robin Story Book.* Complete sets of first American editions of the Pooh books in jacket are very rare in any condition, hence the **$2,500** price at auction.

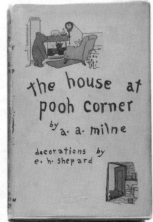

Image courtesy Heritage Auctions

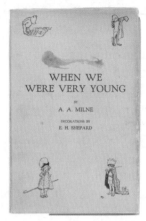

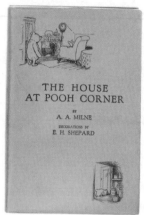
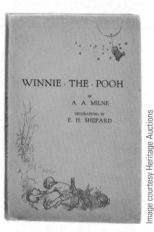

First Edition Set of Winnie-the-Pooh

by A.A. Milne. Unsigned, London: Methuen & Co., 1924-1928.

Includes *When We Were Very Young, Winnie-the-Pooh, Now We Are Six* and *The House at Pooh Corner.* It brought **$5,938** at auction – not bad for unsigned copies, definitely enticing to an advanced collector or a passionate lover of our favorite Bear Of Little Brain.

A. A. Milne, first American Editions of all of the "Pooh" books and The Christopher Robin Story Book,

New York: E. P. Dutton & Co., Inc., 1924-1929.

Titles include: *When We Were Very Young; Winnie-the-Pooh; Now We Are Six; The House at Pooh Corner; The Christopher Robin Story Book* (not pictured). Together, five small volumes. Complete sets of first American editions of the Pooh books in jacket are very rare in any condition. **$2,500**

Winnie the Pooh and Eeyore
Production Cel (Walt Disney, 1980s/90s).

Featuring Winnie-the-Pooh, Piglet, Rabbit, Owl, Kanga and Roo, Eeyore, Rabbit, Tigger, and Christopher Robin, this cel sold for **$956** at auction.

Image courtesy Heritage Auctions

Winnie the Pooh and the Honey Tree
Movie poster (Buena Vista, 1966), 27" x 41".

This was the movie that first brought the Pooh bear and his friends to the big screen. It also introduced many of us to the phrase "rumbly in my tumbly". **$191**

Winnie the Pooh Illustration
By Chris Dellorco (Walt Disney, 1990s).

Disney artist Dellorco created this for consumer product use. It sold for **$84** at auction.

Image courtesy Heritage Auctions

JESSIE WILLCOX SMITH

A Child's Garden of Verses

This delightful piece hails from one of Jessie Willcox Smith's most important projects, *A Child's Garden of Verses*. The illustration is masterfully composed and the swirling composition is one of her most intricate. It is nothing less than a glowing celebration of childhood – and motherhood. This illustration appeared on page 116 of Robert Louis Stevenson's book. Smith's unparallel talent for figure painting with personality is on full display in this charming group portrait. No surprise when this brought **$310,700** when it appeared at auction – something that is not likely to happen again anytime soon.

Image courtesy Heritage Auctions

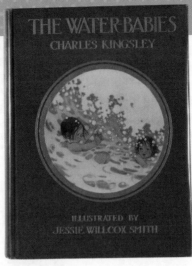

The Water-Babies
by Charles Kingsley, Jessie Willcox Smith, illustrator, New York: Dodd, Mead, 1916.

First Edition of Kingsley's incredibly popular early 20th century book, illustrated with 12 color plates by Willcox Smith. A near fine copy of this is a steal at auction for **$56** and a treasure on any bookshelf.

Image courtesy Heritage Auctions

Whether you know it or not, that picture in your head of the perfect child and the perfect childhood comes to us from Jessie Willcox Smith, one of the greatest pure illustrators the world has ever seen. Her stylized, impeccable artwork "pictured a child that was without equal in reality – innocent, unblemished, never naughty, always perfect," in the words of biographer S. Michael Schnessel. We couldn't agree more.

Her portraits were no less than masterful, always delightful and composed beyond measure. Her simplest drawings were masterpieces of intricacy and always nothing less than a radiant, rosy celebration of the very idea of childhood itself.

Willcox Smith studied under Thomas Eakins at the Pennsylvania Academy of the Fine Arts in the late 1800s, before finding work at *Ladies' Home Journal.* At the end of her stint there she famously continued her art education, studying with Howard Pyle, first at Drexel and then at the Brandywine School. After that, illustrating stories for the most important magazines of the day –Harper's, McClure's, Scribner's and the Ladies' Home Journal – her skills were razor sharp and her reputation was made.

She is, perhaps, most famous for her work on Robert Louis Stevenson's *A Child's Garden of Verses*, though we could also make an argument for her *Mother Goose* being the most well-known. Choosing her best work, however, would be like choosing your favorite Beatles song: impossible. Every one of her works contains some gem of genius. As Jessie Willcox Smith biographer S.

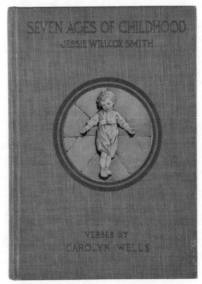

The Seven Ages of Childhood
by Carolyn Wells, Jessie Willcox Smith, illustrator. New York: Moffat, Yard, 1909.

Seven lovely color plates by Smith in this book amply demonstrate her tremendous charm and range. This copy, in good condition, realized **$75** when it sold.

Image courtesy Heritage Auctions

Michael Schnessel has aptly observed, "Jessie Willcox Smith was the creator of the ideal child. She pictured a child that was without equal in reality – innocent, unblemished, never naughty, always perfect. Smith's touching, sensitive portraits of children at play won her the hearts of millions of Americans."

Collecting Willcox Smith is relatively easy, as there are plenty of volumes bearing her name and work making the rounds of used bookstores, dealers and auctions, all of which can be had for anywhere between $10-$50 depending on the title and the edition. Her original art, however, is another story. As one of the greatest illustrators in history, her work is going to bring $5,000+ for minor illustrations and hundreds of thousands for the very best – worth every cent, in our humble observation.

A Child's Prayer (1925)

This Jessie Willcox Smith masterpiece, the cover for *A Child's Prayer* (1925), sold for **$112,500** a few years ago and would likely bring well more than that today. This illustration captures everything that is great about Willcox Smith. This interior illustration of a child sleeping from the same book sold for **$6,563** at auction while the illustration of two children praying sold for **$5,000** at auction.

Image courtesy Heritage Auctions

The Jessie Willcox Smith Mother Goose

Jessie Willcox Smith, illustrator, New York, Dodd, Mead & Company, 1914.

First American edition. The 17 full-page illustrations inserted throughout this book rank among Willcox Smith's most beloved and well known. This copy, a little worse for wear and tear, but still very good, sold for **$250**.

Image courtesy Heritage Auctions

AN ABUNDANCE OF RICHES

(1940-1959)

The world of Children's Books, defined between 1940 and 1959, is possibly the richest in the history of the form. So many great names and great books emerged in the middle of the 20th century that an encyclopedia dedicated just to this period would not be able to fully encompass the excellence that emerged.

The Second World War once again set the world on its heels, but in the healing that followed there arose, in literature aimed at kids, a uniquely compassionate and direct way of speaking to them. This was ever-present in Margaret Wise Brown's *Goodnight Moon*, in H.A. Rey's *Curious George* and in the parable nature of C.S. Lewis's *Chronicles of Narnia*. The voices of the great writers and artists of the time longed for a simpler world, but they could not un-see what they had seen and lived through. The desire to speak directly to children, about both the magic of life and the harsh nature of the world – to comfort as well as to warn – was irresistible.

We had survived our greatest threat to date, defeating a pronounced and obvious evil in the form of Hitler and the Axis powers, but the cost of that victory came in the form of the atom bomb, in the form of millions of deaths across the battle theaters of Europe and Asia. Here was proof, if ever it was presented, that there was no safe place, not even in the idylls of childhood. If it is not mistrust of adults that emerges in the great children's books of the time, it is a distinct wariness of their actions. The principal figures in stories became the children themselves, often paired with animals. Where an adult perspective was necessary, that perspective was minimized, made to take a backseat, or metamorphosed into an entirely different creature that, while adult, was not necessarily human (Dr. Seuss, anyone?).

Things would never be the same. American hegemony was basically unchallenged in the two decades after the war. Technology, industry and innovation were sewing the seeds of a cultural revolution that would dismantle that hegemony even as American Pop Culture rose to lord monolith-like over the tastes of children. That powerful fruit would flower in the mid-and-late-1960s.

The children that benefited from the new wave of children's authors publishing between 1940 and 1959, empowered like never before to think freely and follow flights of imaginative fancy (their own and those of the authors they loved), were learning to view themselves independently of their families, their upbringing and their expected stations in life. Books of the day showed them wisdom, freedom and creativity in a way that had never been experienced before. Focused through the emerging lens of Modernism, a philosophy of art, aesthetics and contemplation that rose with the rapid development of cities and industry, it's no surprise that this was directly reflected in the stories children read.

This was the period of Dr. Seuss, of E.B. White and his *Charlotte's Web*, of *Eloise* and *Harold and the Purple Crayon*, of Saint-Exupery and *The Little Prince*. Powerhouse writers and artists, under the influence of jazz, rock 'n' roll, television and film were breaking open the ways of seeing childhood and relating that experience directly to the children themselves. The middleman in the equation, parents – a necessary thing to buy the books – were not asked for their opinions or input. The results were striking, rich and beautiful. Clearly Children's Books were up to the task of tackling Modernity and the new ways of thinking that accompanied it.

Thidwick the Big-Hearted Moose
by Dr. Seuss, New York: Random House, 1948.
Wonderful First Edition of this very early Seuss book. **$1,434**

Image courtesy Heritage Auctions

Little Fur Family
by Margaret Wise Brown, New York: Harper & Brothers Publishers, 1946.

Original fur slipcover over boards in fine condition, complete with original illustrated box, book illustrated by Garth Williams. **$657** at auction.

Image courtesy Heritage Auctions

Three Little Animals
by Margaret Wise Brown, pictures by Garth Williams. New York: Harper and Brothers, 1956

First edition of a delightful little book, brought **$62** online.

Image courtesy Heritage Auctions

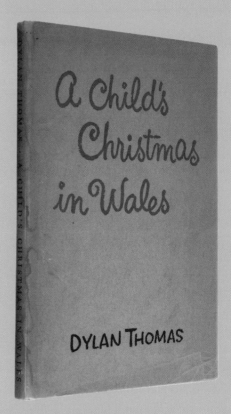

A Child's Christmas in Wales
by Dylan Thomas, New York: James Laughlin, 1954.

This famous Children's Book was published posthumously following the untimely Nov. 9, 1953, death of the Welsh poet, playwright and short-story writer whose unfortunate addiction to alcohol eclipsed even his prodigious literary talent. Expect to pay north of **$200** for a nice edition.

Image courtesy Heritage Auctions

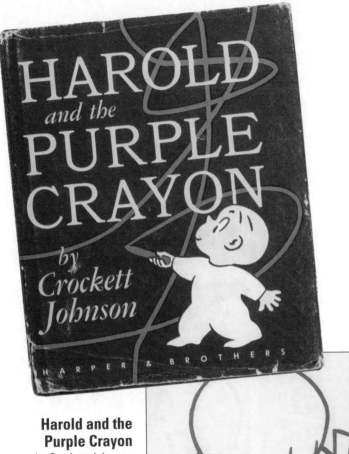

Harold and the Purple Crayon
by Crockett Johnson,
Harper & Brothers,
New York, 1955.

First Edition. The first of
Harold's adventures with his
magical crayon, still widely
read and beloved, which won
the 1956 Caldecott Medal.
You can tell it's a first edition
because it does not have the
Caldecott seal. **$1,020**

Image courtesy Justin Benttinen/
PBA Galleries.

And he landed the balloon on the grass in
the front yard.

66 My favorite book when I was a
kid was Harold and the Purple Crayon
by Crockett Johnson. I loved the
simplicity of it, I guess, as it was one
of the first books I could read by
myself. But more, I loved the simplicity
of the concept: that a kid could have
a crayon that would draw the world
around him. What power! It's the
ultimate kid fantasy, isn't it? That
you are entirely in control, when, in
fact, you aren't in control at all... I
loved the moose that ate the pies and
the mountain that turned into a cliff
and I especially loved the big city,
and, of course, the tender ending, that
all a kid really wants is to be safe in
his own bed. This awesome book also
served as a teething ring for one of
my kids, so I have a lovingly chewed
copy in my library. 99

GARTH STEIN is the author of four novels, including
the *New York Times* bestselling "A Sudden Light" and
the international bestselling, "The Art of Racing in the
Rain." He is co-founder of Seattle7Writers.org. He lives
in Seattle with his wife and no-longer-teething children.

Photo courtesy Susan Doupé Photography

CHRONICLES OF NARNIA

C.S. Lewis' (1898-1963) *Chronicles of Narnia* is a profoundly influential series of children's books. The seven fantasy books that Lewis wrote across the course of seven years were not only the most widely read and acclaimed of Lewis' remarkable career, the books still rank among the most popular fantasy books in the world, period, second only to J.R.R. Tolkein's *The Lord of the Rings* trilogy (Tolkein and Lewis were good friends). For our money, *Narnia* is also much more accessible to children in terms of its writing, its themes and its characters.

The books concern the lifespan of the universe of Narnia, as seen

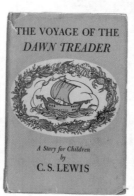

The Chronicles of Narnia

by C. S. Lewis, New York, The MacMillan Co., 1950-1956.

First American editions, including *The Lion, The Witch and the Wardrobe, Prince Caspian, The Voyage of the Dawn Treader, The Silver Chair, The Horse and His Boy, The Magician's Nephew* and *The Last Battle*. Illustrated by Pauline Baynes. A good set that brought **$1,875** at auction.

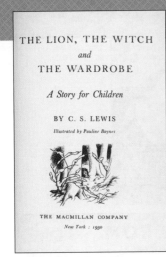

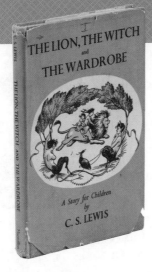

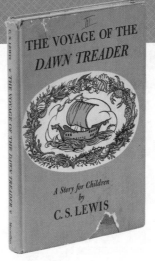

through the eyes of the four Penvensie children, who are called upon by the world's mysterious, mythical savior Aslan The Lion (described by Lewis as an incarnation of what Jesus Christ may have appeared as in an alternate universe) to save Narnia at various points in its history. While the children's various visits to Narnia take place across an unspecified span of many centuries in the fantasy world, they live "normal" lives in 1940s England.

There are many deep and thoughtful insights that Lewis presented in *Narnia*, including meditations on war and racism, what makes the series standout is its treatment of religion. Very few books of the mid-20th century (or after, for that matter) deal with matters of faith with such pertinent allegory. Lewis was a convert to Christianity in his later life and his faith, as relayed in Narnia via Aslan, his figurehead, is as nuanced and practical as it is mysterious and cryptic.

While the books really did not need the help, they were given a bump in the popular imagination in the form of three films based on the first three books, with a fourth film due in the next few years. For collectors, expect to pay upwards of $1,500+ for a complete set of first editions of the *Narnia* books, though good sets and individual copies of later editions can be had across the price spectrum.

The first three stories from Lewis's Chronicles of Narnia Series by C.S. Lewis
First American Editions, 1950-52. Macmillan, New York.

Includes: *The Lion, The Witch, and The Wardrobe*, 1950, *Prince Caspian*, 1951 and *The Voyage of the Dawn Treader*, 1952. Three volumes, original cloth and pictorial dust jackets. First American editions. **$960**

Image courtesy of Justin Benttinen/PBA Galleries.

The Chronicles of Narnia: The Lion, the Witch and the Wardrobe (Buena Vista, 2005) One Sheet
An unused, un-restored poster like this, well-stored and kept, brought **$20** in an online auction, quite affordable for fans of the popular Narnia films.

Image courtesy Heritage Auctions

LITTLE GOLDEN BOOKS

The complete history of Little Golden Books is enough to fill a book of its own. In fact, several books have already been written on the history of these wonderful little books with foil spine. As this is a celebration of the whole of children's books, Little Golden Books can hardly be overlooked even if their place in history has already been recognized.

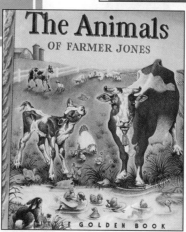

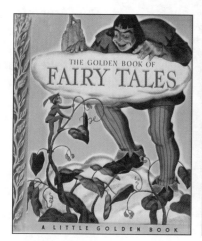

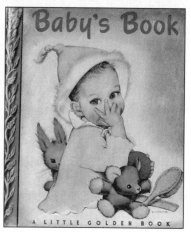

Little Golden Books

The first 12 Little Golden Books, published by Little Golden Books, Oct. 1942. First editions of these classics will run you anywhere from **$50-$300** at auction or online, depending on condition.

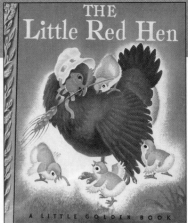

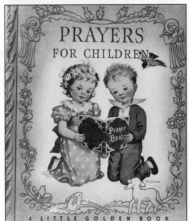

We like to think of Little Golden Books as the great equalizer. When Western Publishing debuted Little Golden Books in the early 1940s, the success was immediate. The first dozen, featuring the ever-popular *Poky Little Puppy,* were cheap to make, used little paper, were durable in the hands of children and – best of all – they were inexpensive, a very popular feature given the frugality the war years necessitated.

Little Golden Books can trace their beginning to the Great Depression and Western's introduction of the first Big Little Book – *The Adventures of Dick Tracy.* Big Little Books provided cheap entertainment to cash-strapped consumers in the early 1930s, proving ever-more popular as the years passed. As the Depression ended, Western signed a contract with Disney allowing them to feature Disney's biggest character - a stroke of genius on behalf of both companies. Further collaborations with Simon & Schuster and Dell Publishing were to come.

With the conception of Little Golden Books, and the first 12 titles, the wheels were set in motion for a juggernaut that still continues chugging to this day. We all read

Little Golden Books as kids, and all of our children read them somewhere, at some point. It's an American Rite of Passage.

Collecting Little Golden Books can be a tremendously entertaining pursuit, and re-reading them will certainly induce a good bit of nostalgia. Given then these books were published in such large numbers, it makes it fairly easy to pick up first editions of the original 12 for between $50 and $200, depending on the title and the condition. Edition number is easy enough to determine by looking on page one or two of the book. If you don't want to spend hundreds, you can also pick up excellent groupings of later edition Little Golden Books for as little as dollar or two apiece, about what you'd pay buying them off the shelf.

Farm Stories, A Giant Golden Book illustration
Gustaf Tenggren (American 1896 - 1970), 1946.

Gouache on board, 14 x 22 in. Signed lower right. This illustration appeared in Kathryn Jackson's children's book, *Farm Stories*, Simon and Shuster, 1946. **$1,912**.

Image courtesy Heritage Auctions

CHARLOTTE'S WEB

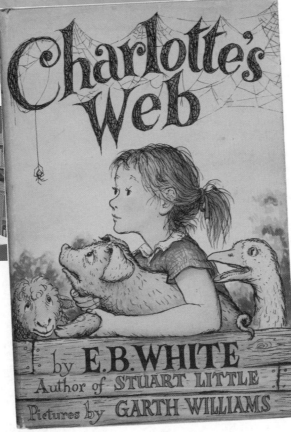

Charlotte's Web
by E.B. White, New York: Harper
& Brothers, Publishers, 1952

Wonderful copy of the first edition,
illustrations by Garth Williams.
$3,250 at auction.

Image courtesy Heritage Auctions

Published by Harper & Brothers in 1952, *Charlotte's Web* by E.B. White and illustrated by Garth Williams, really needs nothing else said about it beside that, in 2000, *Publisher's Weekly* named it the best-selling children's paperback book of all time.

This amazing book is the entire package. Want to show a child what truly great writing looks and reads like? This is the book. Want to show a child the true potential of brilliant illustration? This is the book. Want to speak directly, openly and compassionately about life, death and struggles in-between? This is the book.

Charlotte's Web concerns the life of one Wilbur the pig, the runt of his litter and the object of the affections of the young girl, Fern, whose father intends to slaughter Wilbur soon after his birth. Wilbur is befriended by the spider, Charlotte, who helps save his life via some timely messages spun in her web. Soon the friendship between pig and spider is cemented, and Wilbur finds himself one famous pig. Charlotte dies at the end of the book, in one of the saddest scenes in all of literature, but leaves Wilbur with the legacy of her children and with his eternal gratitude for the kindness she showed him.

Charlotte's Web was one of the very first books to speak directly about the realities of life and death to children. The narrative and the characters are unsparing, with deep pathos, but the book is also very clear in its messages of love and friendship and, with every word, is a simple wonder to behold and a joy to read.

MY FAVORITES:
1940-1959

Little Bear by Else Holmelund Minarik, illustrated by Maurice Sendak (1957):

If ever there was a book version of comfort food, then Little Bear is it. Sendak's scrumptiously sophisticated illustrations of the anthropomorphized Bear Family along with Minarek's simply poetic, comforting prose make for a mainstay of childhood. This is the inaugural title in the I Can Read series published by HarperCollins (previously Harper & Bros.), now comprising hundreds of titles to serve beginning readers. There are five great books in the original Little Bear series all illustrated by Sendak; a sixth written two years before Minarek's death in 2010 is illustrated by Dorothy Doubleday.

The Borrowers by Mary Norton (1952):

The story of the Clocks, a family of "borrowers," a tiny people who live by "borrowing" things from big people. The inventive ways they create all their furniture and tools from big people things is fascinating enough, but soon the daughter makes friends with a human — the worst possible breaking of the rules — and all kinds of fun ensues. The adventures continue across five books.

The Carrot Seed
by Ruth Krauss, illustrated by
Crockett Johnson (1945):

Simple text, simple pictures, big message equals a masterpiece. A beautiful work of encouragement to little ears; sometimes you just have to believe to persevere, even without the support of those closest to you.

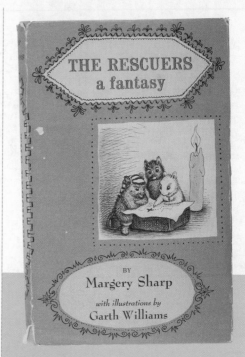

The Rescuers by Margery Sharp (1959):

Did you see the 1977 Disney movie? If that's all you remember, prepare to be blown away by this stunningly poignant adventure tale that is far superior. Three mice are on a wild journey to rescue a Norwegian poet imprisoned in the Black Tower. So much deeper than the film and a must-read.

Henry Huggins by Beverly Cleary (1950):

Having read and loved every one of Cleary's books, I'm claiming this as my favorite. I remember loving the story of how Henry finds the stray Ribsy, smuggles him on a bus to get him home, talks his parents into keeping him and then has to fight for him when Ribsy's first owner shows up. This is where the saga of Klickitat Street begins. Cleary books endure due to the respect she has for her audience.

Pippi Longstocking
by Astrid Lindgren (1945):

Lindgren's enduring character was created by the author to entertain her sick daughter. I fell under the spell of Pippi Longstocking at the age of eight and my daughter followed suit. The magic formula: Pippi lives all alone, is independently wealthy, completely unaware of social etiquette and has superhuman strength. Perhaps Pippi is not the best role model but she'll always stick up for the underdog, and her friendship with Tommy and Annika — the "proper" children next door — helps to keep her grounded.

Caps for Sale: A Tale of a Peddler, Some Monkeys and Their Monkey Business
by Esphyr Slobodkina (1940):

Slobodkina, a Russian immigrant, was a founding member of the American Abstract Artists group and began her children's book career to supplement her income, illustrating many Margaret Wise Brown books. This folktale is retold with lilting repetition and rich, stylized illustrations. Monkeys making mischief is always pleasing, no matter how old you are.

The Twenty-One Balloons
by William Pène du Bois (1947/1948 Newberry winner):

This odd story captivated me when I was young, and decades later my daughter was equally entranced. Pene du Bois takes the historical explosion of the island of Krakatoa in 1883 and weaves the wonderfully imaginative tale of Professor Sherman, whose hot air balloon crashes on the island, just days before it explodes. It's there he finds the small, secret, intricately organized society — wondrous houses, gourmet food, and a well-rehearsed escape plan — that makes this book so special. And the inventions! The idea of beds rising through the roof for sleeping under the stars has stuck with me all these years.

Harold and the Purple Crayon
by Crockett Johnson (1955):

Johnson's innovative and beloved tale invites us to follow young Harold on a creative journey. I was always impressed by Harold's ability to take risks while using common sense to escape danger as he improvises the world around him. In the end, he is back at home, safe, in bed. Johnson and his wife Ruth Krauss, author of *The Carrot Seed*, made an interesting pair, influencing generations and even mentoring Maurice Sendak.

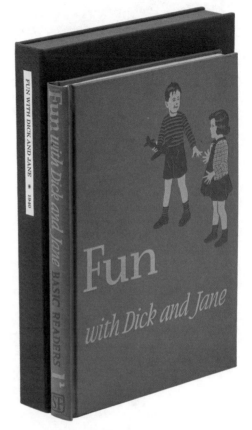

Fun With Dick and Jane
by Williams S. Gray & May Hill Arbuthnot, Scott, Foresman and Company, Chicago, 1942.

First Edition. A fine copy of this popular reader, which brought **$192** at auction. The *Dick and Jane* books were incredibly popular in their day, acting as reading primers for countless thousands of American children.

Image courtesy Justin Benttinen/PBA Galleries

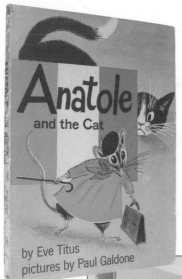

Anatole and the Cat

by Eve Titus, Paul Galdone, illustrator, London: The Bodley Head Co., 1958.

A Caldecott Honor Book, beautifully illustrated and quite popular in its day. Time has not kept this book front of mind, however, and first editions like this can be found for about **$45** online. Newer editions go down in price accordingly.

Image courtesy of eBay, seller: lasting479.

Many Moons

by James Thurber, Harcourt Brace & Company, NY, 1943.

First Edition, first printing. Winner of the Caldecott Medal, illustrated with numerous color drawings by Louis Slobodkin. Concerning the ailing Princess Lenore and the one thing that will make her better: the moon. This edition, in very good condition, is available online for around **$40**.

Image courtesy of eBay, seller: u.s.smitty

Ape in a Cape, an Alphabet of Odd Animals

by Frtiz Eichenberg, Harcourt Brace, 1952.

First Edition of this little-remembered Caldecott Honor Book. Easily obtainable online in the **$10** price range.

Image courtesy of eBay, seller: jcheyne.

The Little Prince
by Antoine de Saint-Exupéry, New York:
Reynal & Hitchcock, 1943.

First Edition in English, translated from the French by Katherine Woods with illustrations by the author. A beautiful little book that works in whatever language it's been translated into, which is almost every single one. In Very Good condition like this, any lover of this book would count themselves lucky to pick it up at auction for **$1,150**.

Image courtesy Heritage Auctions

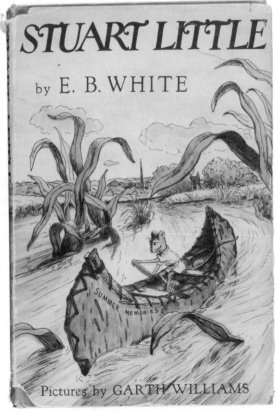

Stuart Little
by E.B. White, New York:
Harper & Brothers, 1945.

First Edition, first printing, inscribed by White on the half-title page, "For Max / from E B White." Illustrated by Garth Williams and signed by him in pencil on the lower margin of the frontispiece. This copy, with White's signature, brought **$3,500** at auction. This is still a popular book, delightful in many ways and surreal in so many others. Still compelling, we have to admit that, reading this as adults, the book leaves the reader scratching their heads a bit, owing to Stuart's disjointed adventures and the abrupt ending.

Image courtesy Heritage Auctions

The Big Golden Book of Elves and Fairies
by Jane Werner, New York: Golden Press, 1951.

Illustrated by Garth Williams. **$69**

Image courtesy Heritage Auctions

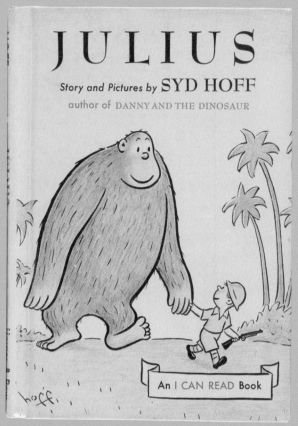

Julius
by Syd Hoff, New York: Harper & Row, ca. 1959.

Later edition, inscribed by Hoff with an original sketch of a dog. Hoff was, and is, a very popular author, though there are very few examples of his work selling at auction. We suspect this is because the books have all been read until they fell apart. The inscription on this one helped bring the price to **$100**.

Image courtesy Heritage Auctions

CURIOUS GEORGE

Curious George, by H.A. and Margaret Rey, is a perennial classic, and one that has been helped along the way since its inception by various film versions and, these days, by the wonderful PBS Kids version of the character, which is much gentler and more in-tune with children than the original ever was.

That is not to say that the first George book, published in 1941 – and based on a character in the Reys' 1939 book *Cecily G. and the Nine Monkeys* – is not great in its own right. It is indeed, in its wonderful, childlike perspective, though it's hard to see it through modern sensibilities and not feel like George is constantly put in bad situations not at all of his own doing, and yet somehow is blamed for it.

Really. Here you have a little monkey, hanging out in the jungle. He's captured by a Man in Yellow, told he is going to live in a zoo and then is left alone in New York City with a simple "don't get in trouble." To our thinking, The Man in the Yellow Hat is the culpable one here.

At any rate, *Curious George* – along with the other six *George* books in the original run: *Curious George Takes a Job* (1947), *Curious George Rides a Bike* (1952), *Curious George Gets a Medal* (1957), *Curious George Flies a Kite* (1958), *Curious George Learns the Alphabet* (1963), *Curious George Goes to the Hospital* (1966) – is still wildly entertaining, with wonderfully kinetic art, and fully deserving of its place in the pantheon of great children's books.

Curious George
by H.A. Rey, Boston: Houghton Mifflin, 1941.

First edition, original dust jacket with **$1.75** price. This is a crisp, bright copy in near fine condition, extremely scarce, which brought **$26,290** at auction. This is a top shelf book for the serious collector showing one of the pinnacles of Children's literature. *Curious George* has remained immensely popular through thousands of printings and dozens of iterations on film and television around the world. We have to say that the PBS Curious George cartoon of the early 2000s was a wonderful interpretation of the books, updating the character, making the stories gentler and more accessible.

Image courtesy Heritage Auctions

How The Grinch Stole Christmas!

by Dr. Seuss,
Random House,
New York, 1957.

Released in December of 1957, this holiday favorite is illustrated throughout by the author, Theodor "Dr. Seuss" Geisel. *School Library Journal* named it one of the Top 100 Picture Books of All-Time in 2012. This first edition, first printing sold for **$390**.

Images courtesy Justin Benttinen/ PBA Galleries.

...HE HIMSELF...!
The Grinch carved the roast beast!

Three thousand feet up! Up the side of Mt. Crumpit,
He rode with his load to the tiptop to dump it!
"Pooh-Pooh to the *Whos!*" he was grinch-ish-ly humming.
"They're finding out now that no Christmas is coming!
"They're just waking up! I know *just* what they'll do!
"Their mouths will hang open a minute or two
"Then the *Whos* down in *Who*-ville will all cry BOO-HOO!

For more on Dr. Seuss see page 196.

You're a mean one, Mr. Grinch. But we still love you, as evidenced by the sale of this rare ink-and-paint color model cel for **$3,100** at auction. The cel, from the animated TV classic *Dr. Seuss' How The Grinch Stole Christmas*, is on acetate and measures 16" x 12", perhaps the largest cel of the Grinch ever produced.

ROBERT MCCLOSKEY

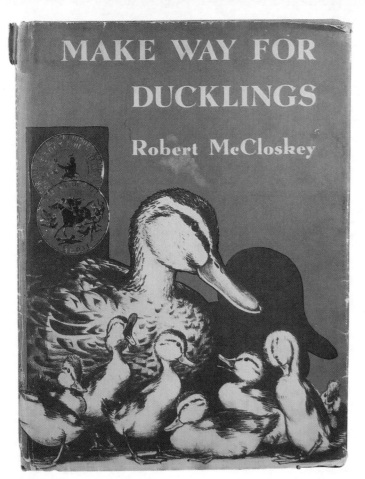

We find Robert McCloskey to be an amazing illustrator and author – certainly one of the most popular of his day. While many of his books are no longer in print, his masterpieces are certainly still easy to find in stores, online and at auction. The most endearing of these books, *Make Way For Ducklings*, is still completely charming, though we have to admit that *Blueberries for Sal* is our favorite, with its lovely little protagonist, its idyllic setting and its delightful conclusion.

Make Way for Ducklings
by Robert McCloskey, New York: The Viking Press, 1941.

First edition, first printing. This Caldecott Medal winner is arguably McCloskey's best and certainly his most widely read. This edition, in the incredibly rare dust jacket, was listed online for **$6,500**, though later printings can be had for much less. Modern copies are usually within the **$10-$15** range.

Image courtesy eBay, seller: Burnside Rare Books.

Blueberries for Sal
by Robert McCloskey, New York: The Viking Press, 1948.

First printing, first edition with a fourth-edition dust jacket. True first editions of this lovely, lilting and heartfelt book by McCloskey are exceedingly rare and would run several thousand dollars. This one was listed online at **$395**, not a bad price for such a fine book. Modern copies can be had for a song at most any bookstore or online.

Image courtesy eBay, seller: grindingguy

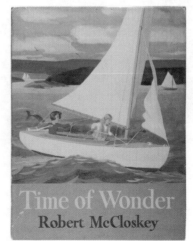

Time of Wonder
by Robert McCloskey, New York: The Viking Press, 1957.

First edition. **$138**

Image courtesy Heritage Auctions

One Morning in Maine
by Robert McCloskey, Viking Press, New York, illustrated by the author, 1952.

First editions of this title are quite scarce, especially in the dust jacket. Well-priced at auction for **$270**.

Image courtesy Justin Benttinen/PBA Galleries

Eloise
by Kay Thompson, New York: Simon and Schuster, 1955

First Edition, first printing, inscribed and signed by the author and the illustrator, Hilary Knight, on the front endpapers. **$1,375**.

Image courtesy Heritage Auctions

Eloise at Christmastime
by Kay Thompson, 1958. Random House, New York.

Illustrated by Hilary Knight. First Edition, first printing. **$120**

Image courtesy Justin Benttinen/PBA Galleries.

GOODNIGHT MOON

Goodnight Moon
by Margaret Wise Brown,
Harper & Brothers, 1947

A very rare true First Edition
of this classic, plus the even
more-scarce original dust
Jacket. This edition sold for
$800 on eBay.

Image courtesy of eBay,
seller: treasuregallery10.

Margaret Wise Brown wrote *Goodnight Moon* in 1947 and, as beloved as the book is today, it didn't become a bona fide classic, or a sales sensation, until the 1970s. In fact, it routinely sold between 10,000 and 20,000 copies a year in its first few decades – respectable, but hardly the gangbuster sales you might expect from one of the greatest picture books of all time (and the very first book we read to our daughter the day she came home from the hospital).

What was it that lit the fire under *Goodnight Moon*? It's impossible to say, but somehow it seems appropriate considering the gentle, sloping ritual of the book, which is in no seeming hurry to get anywhere at all besides the next word and the thing to bid good evening to.

In *Goodnight Moon,* a baby bunny is readying itself for sleep, sitting in its mothers lap, saying goodnight to the various things in the room, including (everyone's favorite) "a comb and a brush and a bowl full of mush." There is gentility, warmth and safety in the ritual between the two and the overall dreamy effect of the book is sweet and lingering, setting the perfect mood for a good night's sleep.

A TURNING POINT

(1960-1979)

The period between 1960 and 1979 represented broad changes in our culture that were unlike any period in history before it. Was it The Beatles and the British Invasion in rock 'n' roll? Was it the Civil Rights Movement? Woodstock? The death of President Kennedy? The Vietnam War? Baby Boomers coming of age?

It was all these things and more – more than we can point to here – that contributed to these shifts. Two centuries of simmering American history and energy – good and bad, repressive and expressive – had finally reached a boiling point and exploded into the world. The sense of well-being brought about by the American century's peak in the 1950s was messily shattered and measured in the clear social schism between right and left, liberal and conservative that emerged.

By the end of the '60s, and through the '70s, the confluence of three generations would occur – The Greatest Generation, which fought World War II, the Baby Boomers, who reaped the spoils of the fight, and Gen-X, born into a society seeing so much change on so many fronts that no one was exactly sure what to do with them – and the results, as far as Children's Books would go, were groundbreaking.

Whatever boundaries – societal and storytelling – still existed after the 1940s and 1950s were all demolished

in this period. All bets were off as far as social mores were concerned – sex, drugs and rock 'n' roll! – and the traditionally downtrodden were suddenly finding their voices in the form of protests, feminism, Civil Rights and more. To some Americans it was terrifying, to some exhilarating. To the creators of children's books it was a chance to not only speak directly to children, but also quite frankly.

No longer was it necessary to try and shelter children from the outside world. The fantastical and creative universes they imagined could be sinister, terrifying, lonely, you name it. The books of the period tackled gender roles (*Free To Be You and Me*), race relations (*The Snowy Day*), bullying and greed (*Charlie and the Chocolate Factory*), along with a host of issues pertaining to the societal change occurring.

Perhaps no book typifies the period better than Maurice Sendak's genius, sublime *Where the Wild Things Are*. While all of Chapter 8 of this book is dedicated to Sendak and his work, it has to be mentioned here. *Wild Things* is, for our money, the most iconic and important children's book of them all. It may not be *your* absolute favorite, and it may not be *ours,* but we're willing to bet that we all know it and love it. Within this beautiful little book is captured the very essence of the childhood experience and within Sendak's lush,

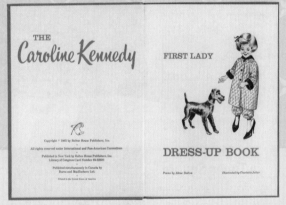

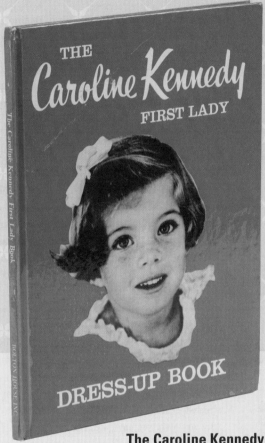

The Caroline Kennedy First Lady Dress-Up Book

by Arlene Dalton, Rolton House Publishers, New York, 1963.

First Edition, first (and only) printing. The ill-fated, seldom-seen Caroline Kennedy book was slated for mass distribution at the same time her father, President John F. Kennedy, was assassinated. Fewer than 1,000 copies were printed. It is doubtful that more than a handful of copies survive. Expect to pay at least **$1,000+** if you want one and can find it.

Images courtesy Justin Benttinen/PBA Galleries

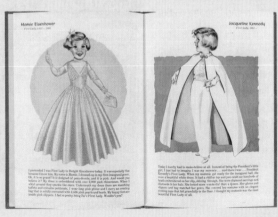

The Adventures of Tom Bombadil and Other Verses from The Red Book

by J. R. R. Tolkien, London George Allen & Unwin, 1962.

First Edition. A rare volume from the legendary author of *The Lord of the Rings*, about one of the great and unsung characters of the first book in *The Lord of the Rings* trilogy. **$179**

Image courtesy Heritage Auctions

The Cricket in Times Square

by George Selden, New York Ariel Books/Farrar, Straus and Cudahy, 1960.

First Edition, first printing, illustrations by Garth Williams. A wonderful copy and a great buy at about **$400** online. This book (and all the Chester Cricket, Tucker Mouse and Harry Cat books) is a perennial favorite in our house. If you've never read any of these, do yourself the favor and pick this book up as soon as possible. You can thank us later.

Image courtesy Heritage Auctions

heartbreaking artwork is the gamut of emotions that this period in children's books encouraged and explored.

Until this time America had managed to maintain a veneer of innocence, a wide-eyed optimism that had powered the nation through its first 200 years of war and political strife. Children's books reflected the sea change in attitudes sweeping popular thinking of the time. Books dealt openly with class-consciousness, poverty, and divorce – subjects that early children's books couldn't even acknowledge. The ideas of the past, the idyllic childhood of summer gardens and fairies and pirates, were dismissed. The epic adventures of *Watership Down*, *The Cricket in Times Square*, *A Wrinkle in Time* and the like told sometimes-terrifying stories of dystopian ideas and severe existential crises.

If the decades took on a darker perspective, they also offered hope for the future. Dr. Seuss's cautionary tale *The Lorax* is the perfect example of this. The book, though set in desolation, ended with hope for the future as the Once-ler drops the last Truffala Tree seed into a boy's hand; Leo Lionni's *Swimmy* navigates the vast ocean on his own, dealing with bullies and finding a group he belongs with – these are profound lessons that so many heroes have to learn. The characters that emerge from the period earn their redemption; they go through the fire, no matter how great or small the story.

These are the hallmarks of an incredible period in the history of Children's Books that has already produced a few bonafide classics and many more that are vying to become so. Only time will tell what survives and what doesn't.

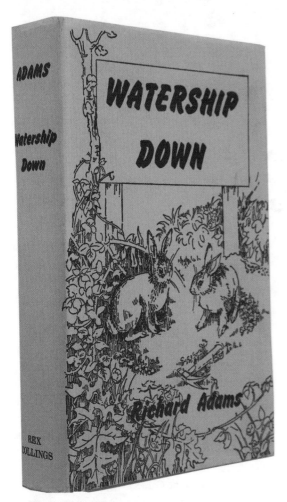

Watership Down

by Richard Adams, London: Rex Collings, 1972.

First Edition, first printing. Adams' tale of rabbit culture was initially turned down by all the major publishing houses, but once it reached the store shelves, it won both the prestigious Carnegie Medal and The Guardian Award for Children's Fiction. Penguin Books reports that *Watership Down* is its best-selling novel of all time. This is an outstanding copy of a scarce modern First Edition. **$3,107** at auction.

Image courtesy Heritage Auctions

Freaky Friday

by Mary Rodgers, New York: Harper & Row, 1972.

Early edition of this 1970s hit, made all the more popular by the Jodie Foster movie of the same name, updated again in the early 2000s with Lindsay Lohan, a version which pales in comparison, in our humble opinion. Easily affordable at auction for **$18**.

Image courtesy Heritage Auctions

THE SNOWY DAY

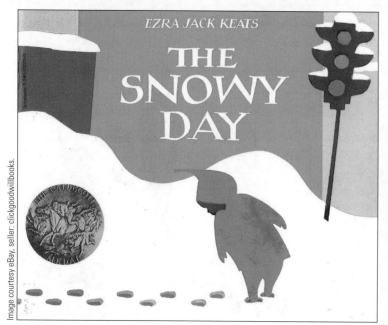

The Snowy Day
by Jack Ezra Keats, New York: Viking Press, 1962

A later edition of Ezra Jack Keats' famous, still incredibly popular *The Snowy Day*, the Caldecott winner in 1963. This book has never been out of print and, where a First Edition can be found, they will generally run on the affordable side, in the range of **$20+**. The one pictured here was listed online for about **$4**. With shipping, it's about what you would pay for a new edition in a store. Keats wrote this, and all his books with incredible compassion and understanding, making it a standard-bearer in the tumultuous 1960s and 1970s as America struggled to reconcile its past and move into the future. While that struggle may still be ongoing, this book remains as beloved and interesting as it ever was.

Ezra Jack Keats' *The Snowy Day* is one of the greatest children's books ever written, for numerous reasons. Published in 1962, it is the story of young Peter as he explores his city neighborhood after the first snowfall of the year. It is an achingly beautiful little book, full of

innocence, wonder and some of the very best, most simple and tightly constructed writing you will encounter anywhere.

Keats, born Ezra Jack Kats in Brooklyn in 1916 and raised Jewish, started illustrating after his service in World War II. After illustrating comics for several years, he was drawn into illustrating children's books in the early 1960s. It was with a keen sense of social justice that he sat down to write *The Snowy Day*, his first book, and the effect was profound. *The Snowy Day* won the Caldecott in 1963.

This wonderful little classic, so beloved now, was quite controversial in its day. Keats, with his hero *Peter*, broke the color barrier in mainstream children's books. It seems a little hard to believe now, given how great the book is, and how great many of Keats' follow-up books were, with several featuring Peter as he grows, but it was a different time. The hindsight we have now, looking back through the American Civil Rights Movement and the progress we have made as a nation, was hard-won by the likes of Keats and his deliberate challenging of the status quo. We owe him a double debt of gratitude: one for his incredible talent and one for his desire to change the world.

Free To Be You And Me
by Marlo Thomas, Bantam, 1974.

A rare First Edition soft cover book and original LP album of this groundbreaking project, funded by the Ms. Foundation and headed up by the inimitable Marlo Thomas. This duo was being offered for **$30** on eBay, though more recent printings can be had for half as much, and the soundtrack — downloadable online — is just as groovy and cool as it was back in the day. *Free To Be…* was groundbreaking in so many ways, not the least of which was its direct addressing of gender stereotyping. Thomas recruited stars of the day to help with the project. Subsequent editions, especially the most recent anniversary edition, are in hardcover and illustrated, making them more appealing to traditional book collectors. As for us, we love both the book and the album.

Image courtesy eBay, seller: foreveryoung!

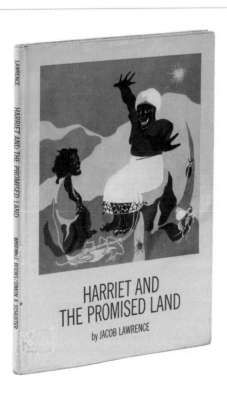

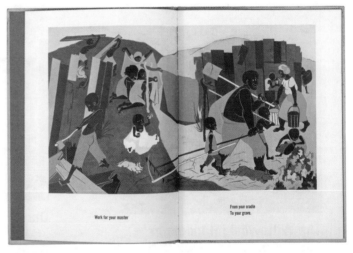

Harriet and the Promised Land
by Jacob Lawrence, Simon and Schuster, Inc., New York, 1968.

First Edition. This is the story of Harriet Tubman, born a slave in Maryland in 1822, who made a daring escape to the North and freedom. At the risk of her life she returned 19 times to lead more than 300 of her people to "The Promised Land." **$180**.

Image courtesy Justin Benttinen/PBA Galleries

Baboushka and the Three Kings

by Ruth Robbins, Nicolas Sidjakov, illustrator, Parnassas, 1961.

First Edition, first printing, with dust jacket. While this book won the Caldecott in 1961, there's not a tremendous amount of First Edition copies around. **$800**. Lesser copies descend in price accordingly.

Image courtesy eBay, seller: harleana.

The Willowdale Handcar or The Return of the Black Doll

by Edward Gorey, New York: Dodd, Mead, 1979.

First Edition, first printing. Not many examples of Gorey selling at auction, but an edition like this brought **$69**.

Image courtesy Heritage Auctions

Once a Mouse

by Marcia Brown, New York: Simon & Schuster Children's Publishing, 1972.

A later edition of this Caldecott winner is pictured here, available for about **$16**. A cute story of a tiger humbled by the magic of an old hermit who reminds the Tiger he started life as a mouse before becoming his royal self.

Image courtesy eBay, seller: grandeagleretail

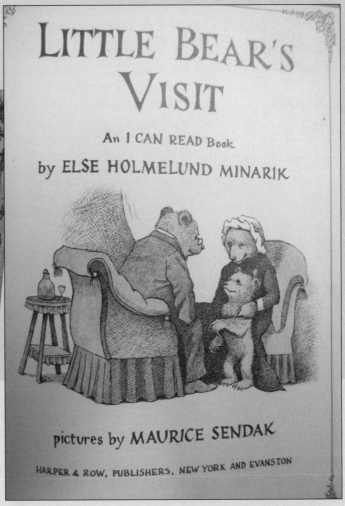

Little Bear's Visit

by Else Holmelund Minarik, Maurice Sendak, illustrator, New York: Harper & Row, 1961.

A First Edition printing, without the dust jacket, of this Cadecott Honor book. The adventures of Little Bear are gentle, compassionate and understanding. Written and drawn in a style that speaks directly to the hearts and minds of children — drawn by Sendak, what do you expect? Depending on condition, expect to pay anywhere from **$20** to **$100+**.

Image courtesy eBay, seller: nimasonry

MY FAVORITES: 1960-1979

The Cricket in Times Square by George Selden, illustrated by Garth Williams (1960):

The tale of the amazing friendship between patient Harry Cat and excitable Tucker Mouse who live together in an abandoned drain pipe in one of the subway stations in Times Square. This magnificent book is made all the more wondrous when they meet Chester Cricket, who manages the impossible: bringing New York City to a complete halt for one brief, perfect moment.

The Phantom Tollbooth by Norton Juster, illustrated by Jules Feiffer (1961):

Milo, bored with his life, comes home to find a tollbooth in his room… In this masterpiece – justly compared to Carroll's *Alice in Wonderland* – Juster takes us to the Lands Beyond for an adventure amidst a feud between the kingdoms of Dictionopolis and Digitopolis. With oodles of puns, word play and number puzzles, Milo frees the Princesses Rhyme and Reason from the Castle in the Air, sets the world straight and vanquishes boredom with an active mind. Sendak's "An Appreciation" in the 50th anniversary edition sums it up perfectly.

A Wrinkle in Time
by Madeline L'Engle (1962):

L'Engle wasn't afraid to explore big issues with young minds in this groundbreaking adolescent science fiction/fantasy tale. We follow awkward 13-year-old Meg Murray on an interstellar journey to find her missing scientist father. Accompanied by her empathic genius young brother, Charles Wallace, popular, loyal Calvin and three fairy godmothers to boot, this adventure is one in which love triumphs and brainy kids are heroes.

Island of the Blue Dolphins
by Scott O'Dell, published in 1960, 1961 (Newbery winner):

Based on a true story from the 19th century, and one of my all-time favorites (I named my childhood dog *Rontu* after the dog in this book!), O'Dell's is a tale of survival *a la* Robinson Crusoe, with a young native girl at its center living alone on one of the Channel Islands off of California. I remember being fascinated at this tale of survival told from a young girl's perspective and inspired by the strength she displays.

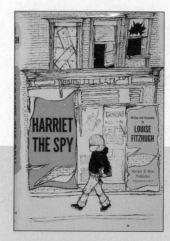

Harriet the Spy by Louise Fitzhugh (1964):

Harriet was like no other girl I had ever encountered in a book before when I met her as a girl. She's an unapologetic rebel who dresses sloppy, wears black glasses without lenses, eats tomato sandwiches, has a nanny named Ole Golly, spies on her neighbors after school and writes about it in her journal. I was blown away. As a child I wasn't aware that parents at the time were up in arms about the "bad example" set by Fitzhugh's anti-heroine.

James and The Giant Peach
by Roald Dahl (1961):

In true Dahl style, the story is as macabre as it is fantastical. James escapes the clutches of his despicable aunts in a magical, giant peach, inhabited by a cast of giant insects. *What?* Dahl makes it work and we gladly follow along.

JAMES AND
THE
GIANT PEACH

A Children's Story

ROALD DAHL

illustrated by
NANCY EKHOLM BURKERT

Alfred A. Knopf: New York

Free To Be You and Me
by Marlo Thomas and friends (1974):

Perhaps the only book to grow out of a record album, it could only be done in the 1970s, right? Both the album and book were a groundbreaking collection of stories, poetry, art and music from the best and brightest of the time. This project challenged stereotypes and envisioned a world where children could grow up unencumbered by unrealistic expectations. We've come far as a society with a long way to go, making this work invaluable to have at home.

Frog and Toad are Friends
by Arnold Lobel (1970):

By turns hilarious, touching and slapstick, Lobel tells the story of a timeless friendship that's never cloying. Temperamental Toad and patient Frog support each other through various misadventures, from eating too many cookies, to losing buttons, to being scared. They bumble their way through their adventures and we see a part of ourselves in each of them.

From the Mixed-Up Files of Mrs. Basil E. Frankweiler
by E.L. Konigsburg (1967):

Claudia, the 12-year-old protagonist, feels bored and under-appreciated, so she talks her younger brother into running away…wait for it…to New York City's Metropolitan Museum of Art. Konigsburg makes this tale of two runaways, narrated by the 82-year-old Mrs. Frankweiler, come alive by providing every detail a kid could want about living inside a museum and then adding in a mystery for the children to solve. A fun adventure with brains.

The Best Christmas Pageant Ever
by Barbara Robinson (1971):

Through narration *a la* the movie "A Christmas Story," Beth Bradley tells us the tale of the Christmas that the Herdmans, the bad seeds of the town, participate in the community Christmas pageant. The Herdmans are over-the-top bullies, but she treats them with empathy and, via their holiday transformation, we're rewarded with a story that is just right.

Mrs. Frisby and the Rats of NIMH
by Robert C. O'Brien (1971):

Mrs. Frisby, a widowed field mouse, needs help saving her home from the farmer's plow. She ends up calling upon a group of rats living nearby and discovers they have developed an advanced society. Told with detail, grace and respect for rats, who are so often the villains of childhood tales.

Sam Bangs and Moonshine

by Evaline Ness, Holt, Rinehart Winston, 1968.

An early edition of the 1969 Caldecott winner. Copies of this book, from first printings up through modern re-issues, will run you in the **$10-$15** range.

Image courtesy eBay, seller: coolbres

Swimmy

by Leo Lionni, New York: Random House, 1963.

A later edition, showing this book as a Caldecott Honor book. Lionni's enchanting drawings are always engaging and the story of a young fish navigating the wide ocean, and outsmarting a bully along the way, is a timeless tale. Copies of this book can be found online for anywhere from **$5** up to **$25+**, depending on the edition.

Image courtesy eBay, seller: goodwillsoutherncalifornia12

May I Bring A Friend?

By Beatrice Schenk de Regniers, Beni Montressor, Illustrator, Athenuem, 1964.

This later edition of *May I Bring A Friend?* represents just one of many copies of this Caldecott-winning book from different printings throughout the last 50 years that are readily available for as little as **$5** and as much as **$40+**. An absurd comedy of manners with Montressor's brilliant illustrations.

Image courtesy eBay, seller: wordery-specialst

A Wrinkle in Time

by Madeline L'Engle, New York: Ariel Books/Farrar, Straus and Cudahy, 1962.

First Edition, first printing with a bookplate signed by the author laid in. This copy brought **$3,500** at auction. A profound and absorbing book, a Newberry winner and a beginner's treatise on Quantum Physics, Existentialism and Eastern Philosophy. Want to introduce BIG concepts to little kids? Give them this book. Want to thrill yourself with a great yarn and a superb adventure that holds up 50 years after it was written? This is the one. Lesser copies can be had at lesser prices, which I encourage any collector to snap up if you see it.

Image courtesy Heritage Auctions

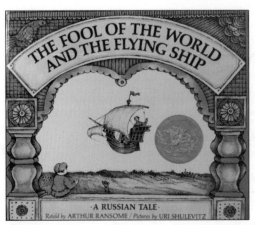

The Fool of the World and The Flying Ship

by Arthur Ransome, Uri Shulevitz, Illustrator, Farrar, Straus & Giroux, 1968.

A 1980s edition of the 1969 Caldecott winner about a man who brings a flying ship to try and win the hand of the Czar's daughter. Easily picked up online for a few dollars. This one was up for **$5** in an online auction.

Image courtesy eBay, seller: qualitybargainbooks

> " I can't choose just one favorite book, but I can choose a favorite reading moment: I was on vacation with my children, ages 4 and 7. They were in a phase where they were not getting along very well. I was reading A Wrinkle in Time to them, sitting on a log by an idyllic little lake at sunset. When I got to the line, "I love you Charles Wallace!" I began blubbering, so moved was I at the power of love between those siblings in the story. My children gaped at me in horror, but how could I explain? "

SONYA SONES is the author of six novels in verse for teens and adults, most recently To Be Perfectly Honest. She lives in Southern California.

ROALD DAHL

Roald Dahl wrote a lot of very good books for both children and adults, but none have stood the test of time as well as the surreal, wonderful, cruel and unpredictable *Charlie and the Chocolate Factory*. It's the ultimate fantasy for kids and the ultimate

Charlie and The Chocolate Factory

by Roald Dahl, illustrated by Joseph Schindelman, New York: Knopf, 1964.

First Edition, first issue. A beauty of an edition in fantastic condition. It brought **$1,375** at auction.

Charlie and The Great Glass Elevator
by Roald Dahl, Knopf, New York, 1972

First American edition. This book, the further adventures of Charlie Bucket and Willy Wonka, was written eight years after the first, but picks up immediately where the first leaves off. We have to say, while the first is a charming and beautiful tale of perseverance and honesty, the second does not live up to the bar set by its predecessor. Dahl chose the second volume to parody politics and the wild world and regional wars affecting the early 1970s. As social satire it's funny, but as a worthy successor to one of the greatest kid's books ever written, it pales. **$192** at auction.

Image courtesy Justin Benttinen/PBA Galleries

&& One of my favorite books as a child was Charlie and the Chocolate Factory, by Roald Dahl. Was? Is. I still have the retro-copy I read when I was 9. As a small person in a big world, it told you the thing you most needed to hear: that a good heart could get you through. It told you other delicious, and downright gleeful things, too. A glint of gold in a chocolate bar could change your life. Bad people could actually get what was coming to them. Charlie Bucket's lessons are both simple and shining — kindness rewards you, and magic awaits you, and an elevator might fly through every kind of glass ceiling. **"**

DEB CALETTI is a National Book Award finalist and award-winning author of more than twelve books for young adults and adults, including Honey, Baby, Sweetheart, Stay, and He's Gone.

Photo courtesy Jason Teeples

morality tale for adults. The structure, characters and writing style is all vintage Dahl and, as with all his books, speaks to all ages of reader.

What is it about the book that has made it a perennial favorite for more than half a century? We think it's in the wonder of the book. It's the fantastic journey of poor, impoverished Charlie Bucket – accompanied by four very bad other children – as a miracle Golden Ticket allows him access to the tightly sealed world of the eccentric chocolate-maker, Mr. Willy Wonka, and – eventually – into ownership of it.

We also think the appeal lies in the book's darkness and frankness. Dahl was one of the first modern children's writers to make his antagonists kids, and not just any old bad kids. The four that accompany Charlie into Wonka's factory are *really* bad.

Willy Wonka & The Chocolate Factory (Paramount, 1971) Poster

Gene Wilder starred as the candy maker in the marvelous movie adaptation of Roald Dahl's *Charlie and The Chocolate Factory*. The film received an Academy Award nomination for Best Original Score and Wilder received a Golden Globe nomination for his work as the eccentric chocolatier Willy Wonka. The movie remains a cult favorite to this day. The poster sold for **$100** at auction.

Image courtesy Heritage Auctions

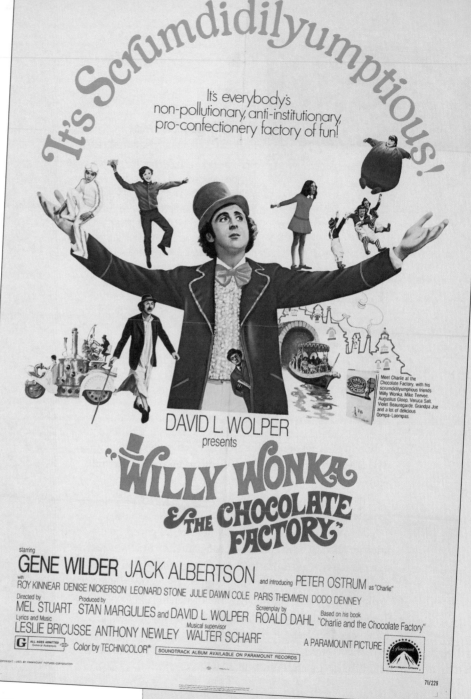

James and The Giant Peach

by Roald Dahl, illustrated by Nancy Ekholm Burkert, New York: Alfred A. Knopf, 1961.

In good condition, **$1,195** at auction.

Image courtesy Heritage Auctions

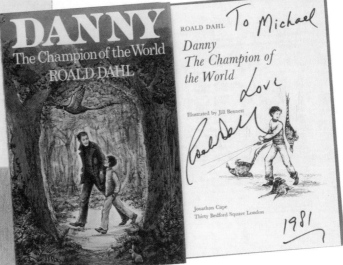

Danny. The Champion of the World

by Roald Dahl, London: Jonathan Cape, 1978.

An early reprint edition inscribed by the author on the title page, illustrated by Jill Bennett. **$194** in an online-only auction.

Image courtesy Heritage Auctions

There is gluttonous August Gloop, spoiled Veruca Salt, impetuous Violet Beauregard and clueless Mike Teevee. They all meet bad ends in the book and they all get their just desserts. The level of retribution Dahl dished out on these characters was just one of the reasons it drew controversy upon publications, but no protest has yet had any impact on the continued popularity of this amazing and always entertaining story.

Published in 1964, *Charlie and the Chocolate Factory* was an immediate hit. It was helped greatly by the 1971 film, *Willy Wonka & The Chocolate Factory,* starring the great Gene Wilder as Wonka. The book has never been out of print and is, thus, easy to find. Expect, however, to pay several hundred dollars for a First Edition.

MAURICE SENDAK

WHERE THE WILD THINGS ARE

SENDAK

WHERE THE WILD THINGS ARE

HARPER & ROW

STORY AND PICTURES BY MAURICE SENDA[K]

Where the Wild Things Are
by Maurice Sendak, New York: Harper & Row, 1963.

First Edition, first issue jacket with **$3.50** price intact and no mention of the Caldecott Award on the jacket flaps, nor with the metallic medal sticker on the front of the jacket. This beauty of a copy sold for more than **$8,400** at auction.

Image courtesy Justin Benttinen/PBA Galleries

In the Night Kitchen
by Maurice Sendak,
Harper & Row, 1970.

A fair price for a signed- copy
of this classic is somewhere
north of **$60**, depending on
the day and who's buying.
Certainly my most favorite
Sendak book (apologies
to *Where the Wild Things
Are*), so wonderfully rich,
entertaining, inscrutable and
infinitely interpretable. Want
to set a child's imagination on
fire? Read them this book!

Image courtesy Heritage Auctions

In der Nachtkuche
(In the Night
Kitchen)
by Maurice Sendak, Diogenes, 1971.

First Edition in German of *In The Night Kitchen*, signed,
with an original drawing by Sendak. **$897**.

Image courtesy Heritage Auctions

Nutshell Library
by Maurice Sendak, Harper & Row, New York, 1962.

Four volumes, which include: *Chicken Soup With Rice,
Pierre, Alligators All Around* and *One Was Johnny*.
Written and Illustrated by Sendak. An early edition signed
by Sendak on front free endpaper. **$420**.

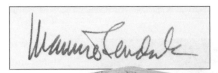

Image courtesy Justin Benttinen/PBA Galleries

For more on Maurice Sendak see page 180.

SHEL SILVERSTEIN

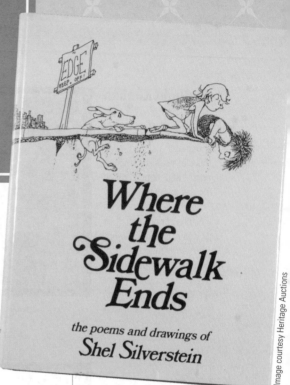

Image courtesy Heritage Auctions

S hel Silverstein (1930-1999) was an American renaissance man. Singer, songwriter, artist, screenwriter, author, Silverstein was an abundantly talented man. He wrote more than 20 books – *The Giving Tree, A Light in The Attic,* to name a few – but it is his work in service of children's poetry that we honor him. When it comes to poems aimed straight at the heart of the modern kid, both in terms of concerns and of fancy, no one did it better than Shel did in his first book of poetry, 1974's *Where The Sidewalk Ends,* published by Harper & Row.

Where The Sidewalk Ends is a collection of 101 sublime poems all from the mind of Silverstein and all wonderfully illustrated with his organic, often heartbreaking and always hilarious style. Every bit of his talent is on display in this superb volume.

From the signature poems of the book (*Invitation, Where The Sidewalk Ends, Boa Constrictor* and *Hug O' War*) to the lesser-known but equally brilliant gems (*Sick, For Sale, Lazy Jane*), the book is a treasury of free-flowing rhyme and sensitive insight. It's no wonder that this is a book that kids read throughout their childhood and well into their adult lives, making it a perennial bestseller of the form and a touchstone of literary awakening.

Good copies of this book are not hard to come by, as it's never been out of print. Expect to pay about cover price for later editions and anywhere from $50 to $100 for a First Edition, more if Silverstein signed it and/or drew a picture in it.

Where the Sidewalk Ends
by Shel Silverstein, New York: Harper and Row, ca. 1982

First published in 1974, this later edition sold at auction for **$21**. Dare we even try and say what this books means to our family? It was one of the earliest and best books of poetry we got our daughter and, when she began reading at an early age, one she read until she had memorized most of them, especially the classic "Sick," which features a "sick" little girl, Peggy Ann McKay, listing the volume of ailments keeping her from going to school — until she realizes it's Saturday.

Falling Up
by Shel Silverstein,
New York: Harper Collins, 1996.

First Edition, second printing. This edition has a two-page illustrated inscription by Silverstein, making it especially desirable and worthy of the **$531** price it commanded at auction.

Image courtesy Heritage Auctions

THE VERY
HUNGRY
CATERPILLAR

by Eric Carle

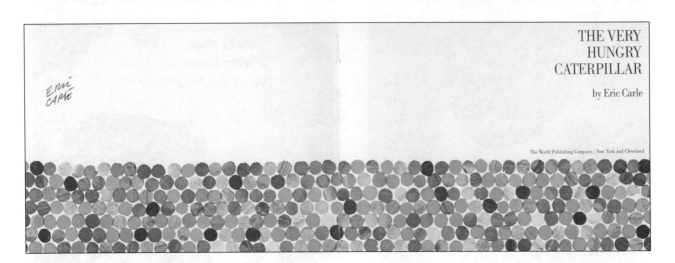

We can not possibly explain the magic of collecting Children's Books without acknowledging Eric Carle. This is the man who wrote *The Very Hungry Caterpillar* in 1969, has illustrated more than 70 books – writing more than 30 of them – and helped make a place for so many of us in early childhood that was a refuge of warmth, color and nature in a complicated world.

Carle, born in Syracuse, N.Y., in 1929, is one of the most prolific kid's authors of all time. His signature collage style art is instantly recognizable. Carle uses hand-painted paper, cut into specific shapes, to create the animals and settings for his book. The effect is a gently charming world that is entirely inviting.

The Very Hungry Caterpillar concerns the title character and his ability to eat *anything* that comes his way, including pickles, ice cream and salami, only to emerge at the end as a beautiful butterfly. It has sold almost 40 million copies and has been translated into more than 58 languages. In 2012, the readers of the *School Library Journal* picked it as the second greatest children's book of all time, second only to *Where The Wild Things Are.* That, friends, is elite company.

The Very Hungry Caterpillar
by Eric Carle, New York: The World Publishing Company, 1969.

An extremely – and I mean *extremely* – rare First Edition of this landmark book, signed by Carle on the page facing the title page. Consider this: More than 38 million copies of this title have been sold. Of those, only a tremendously small amount has survived, especially with the dust jacket, Compound that with the signature and you get an **$11,250** auction price.

Image courtesy Heritage Auctions

Today is Monday
by Eric Carle, Philomel Books, 1993

First Edition, signed by Carle. The book brought **$15**.

Image courtesy Heritage Auctions

Panda Bear, Panda Bear, What Do You See?
by Bill Martin, Jr., Eric Carle, illustrator, New York: Henry Holt, 2003

First Edition, signed by Carle on the title page. **$18**

Image courtesy Heritage Auctions

The Very Clumsy Click Beetle
by Eric Carle, New York: Philomel Books, 1998

First printing with Carle's signature on the title page. **$32**.

Image courtesy Heritage Auctions

Image courtesy Heritage Auctions

Eric Carle, signed, *Hello, Red Fox*
New York: Simon and Schuster, 1998
Second printing, signed by the author. **$44**

Image courtesy Heritage Auctions

The Honeybee and the Robber
by Eric Carle, New York: Philomel, 1981
First Edition, signed by the author. **$75** in an online auction.

" The Very Hungry Caterpillar was one of the first books my son and daughter could "read" along with me by filling in missing words whenever I stopped reading. Did I think they were exceptional? Of course I did! They were able to "read" more and more of the book until my only job was to turn the pages, when they let me. If I asked my kids today (they're in their 20s), I bet they'd remember that the very hungry caterpillar had to eat one nice green leaf before he turned into a beautiful butterfly! I know I did." **"**

AMY SUE NATHAN is the author of *The Good Neighbor* and *The Glass Wives.* She lives in Chicago.

Papa, Please Get the Moon For Me
by Eric Carle, Simon & Schuster Books, 1986

Pictured here is a sixth printing of this beautiful book, signed by Carle on the title page. This one went for **$50** online, a steal.

Image courtesy Heritage Auctions

From Head to Toe
by Eric Carle, HarperCollins, 1997

First Edition, signed by the author on the title page. **$162**

Image courtesy Heritage Auctions

Walter the Baker
by Eric Carle, Simon and Schuster, 1995

Later edition signed by the author. **$81**

Image courtesy Heritage Auctions

"Slowly, Slowly, Slowly," Said the Sloth
by Eric Carle, New York: Philomel Books, 2002

First Edition, signed by the author. Publisher's binding and original dust jacket. Fine. From the collection of Judith Adelman. **$44**.

Image courtesy Heritage Auctions

A SHIFTING LANDSCAPE
(1980-PRESENT)

The period of 1980 to Present is a difficult one to summarize. Is there a through-line in the narratives presented in the last 35 years? Do the authors share a common past, present or vision for the future? Have any books emerged since 1980 that are, without a doubt, unequivocally, classics?

It's impossible to say. What we know is that it's been a very rich few decades in Children's Books. We know that there are probably more books being printed today, by a bigger and more varied group of creators, than ever before, but we also know those books are being printed in ever decreasing numbers – it's the nature of the printing business in a world that has trended decidedly more digital as time has passed.

The last 35 years of Children's Books cannot be seen without viewing them through the lens of technology. More titles, less editions, yes, but modern technology affords writers and artists more platforms than ever to promote their work. The upside is an endless network of exposure.

The downside is that the same technology is available to every person looking to sell a book. How is the germane to this book? It makes predicting what has value and what doesn't much more difficult since a) not enough time has passed to know what books survive in the popular consciousness and b) there are just not very many comparables at auction to measure prices against.

What do we know about the last three decades or so in Children's Books? We know that quality is high but that popularity and staying power is often tied to television and movies. It cannot be helped in the contemporary environment. Would *Harry Potter* have remained a worldwide phenomenon without Hollywood starting the movies before the books were finished? Would the entire resurgence of serial teen fiction have happened at all if it hadn't been for TV and film tie-ins? Would many modern books beloved by kids today be read at all if their readers hadn't seen the movies first (*Shrek,* anyone?)?

The Baby Boomers are now grandparents and Gen-X are parents. Both of these generations are heavy on nostalgia for their youths, which has translated into new life for the books Gen-X read as children and for the books their parents read as children that were then given to Gen-X. These two generations, collectively, have witnessed more change – in society and technology both – than any generation preceding them. The result, as it affects the world of reading and collecting Children's Books, has been a re-trenching in the stories and lessons these generations were weaned on and a serious investment in the books being created by modern artists and writers.

Yes, the march of technology cannot be stopped – and should not be stopped – but there is pronounced movement back to the printed word. We cannot say what specific titles will survive and become classics from today, but we can invest in a future that still honors and regards great storytelling by making them immortal. We do this with our money, our time and our keen interest in the success of the books that are being produced, several of which are detailed on the pages that follow.

Time is the only thing that will provide us a determination of what our greatest stories are. The books we have chosen to include in these pages have all gotten off to a good start. What titles will be venerated 40, 50 and 60 years from now? Given the seismic shifts in attitudes, emotions and technology over the last century it would be foolish to even waste energy thinking about it.

We're all better off just sitting back, cracking open our favorite book with our favorite little person and simply enjoying the story. Isn't this what it's all about, anyway?

No, David!
By David Shannon, Blue Sky Press, 1998.

Later printing, signed and inscribed by the author.
A Caldecott nominee. **$23** online.

Image courtesy Heritage Auctions

Outside Over There

by Maurice Sendak, Harper & Row, New York, 1981.

First Edition, signed by the author on the front free endpaper. Expect to pay in the range of **$150** for an edition like this of Sendak's beautiful and creepy later book.

Image courtesy Justin Benttinen/ PBA Galleries

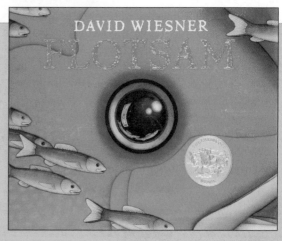

Flotsam
by David Wiesner, New York: Clarion Books, 2006.

No edition stated, signed by the author on the title page. Wiesner's *Flotsam*, a Caldecott Medal winner, is one of the most delightful and intriguing picture books of the last 20 years. A tour de force of imagination and insight, it's a book that's still very popular with the big kid in our house and just one of the fantastic stories that Wiesner seems to routinely unfold. This copy, signed, went for **$15** online, meaning that this is a good time to pick up any copy of this book you see at that price, because it's a classic in the making.

Image courtesy Heritage Auctions

Eragon
by Christopher Paolin, Knopf, 2003.

First Edition, first printing. At auction expect to pay about **$24** for this book, roughly what it would have run you brand new 12 years ago. We can remember this book, the first in the "Inheritance Cycle," being very popular in its day, largely due in part to its author being 15, as well as being bolstered by a feature film with Jeremy Irons that was largely hyped and poorly received by critics.

Image courtesy Heritage Auctions

A Wish for Wings That Work
by Berkeley Breathed, Boston: Little, Brown, 1991.

First Edition, signed by Breathed on the title page. A great Christmas book about Opus the Penguin — one of the greatest comic strip characters ever — from a remarkable talent. **$62** at auction.

Image courtesy Heritage Auctions

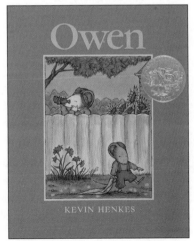

Owen
by Kevin Henke, Greenwillow Books, 1993.

Later printing, signed and inscribed by the author. A Caldecott honor book about Owen, his favorite possession (a yellow fuzzy blanket) and his parents' concerns as Owen readies to begin school. **$15**.

Image courtesy Heritage Auctions

MY FAVORITES: 1980-PRESENT

Sarah, Plain and Tall
by Patricia McLachlan (1985):

I was curious about this slim little book after my daughter's second grade teacher read it to her class. I picked it up, read it in one sitting and it took my breath away. This is a simple tale of love, loss and healing set on the American prairie in the late 1800s, told with poetic grace and authentic emotion. The sequels are good, too!

Lulu's Hat by Susan Meddaugh (2002):

Meddaugh is best known for *Martha Speaks* (which spawned a popular PBS kids cartoon), but this is my favorite of her books. We follow Lulu, adopted into a "True Magic" family, on a summer adventure during which she discovers her true identity. A wildly creative tale that's hard to put down and a nice balance to all the boy wizards and magicians out there.

Madame Pamplemousse and Her Incredible Edibles
by Rupert Kingfisher (2008):

Did you like the movie *Ratatouille*? Then you will love this scrumptiously fun tale of Madeline, whose neglectful parents send her to work in her mean Uncle Lard's kitchen each summer. Things change for everyone when she discovers the amazing Madame Pamplemousse's tiny shop of gourmet treats.

Tumtum and Nutmeg: Adventures Beyond Nutmouse Hall
by Emily Bearn (2008):

It was the cover art that drew me to this book and it didn't disappoint. Big-hearted Mr. and Mrs. Nutmouse live in a 36-room mansion, hidden in the broom closet of Rose Cottage, the home of neglected children Arthur and Lucy. The mouse couple live a quiet and cozy life until they decide to help out the children. You'll thrill to the adventure and surely long to join the Nutmouses for a scrumptious afternoon tea at the mansion.

The Apothecary by Maile Meloy (2011):

I felt like I was 10 again reading this wonderful tale; I just couldn't stop. The setting is 1952 and Janie's parents move her from sunny Southern California to post-World War II London. At her new school she meets the intriguing Benjamin. When his father, the Apothecary, disappears, a wild adventure begins that is tenderly told with respect for its young teenage characters.

The Magical Ms. Plum
by Bonnie Becker (2010):

Becker is best known for her Bear and Mouse picture books – all of which we love – but when I accidentally discovered this little gem, it was a real treat: Ms. Plum captivates her third grade students with her unusual teaching style and her magic supply closet, which somehow seems to give every child just the magic they deserve. A fun tale full of valuable lessons.

Moon Over Manifest
by Clare Vanderpoo (2010):

It's 1936 and twelve-year-old Abilene is sent to stay with her father's friend in Manifest, Kansas. Slowly she makes friends and unravels the mysterious history of the town, discovering where she fits in. This story within a story is intricately woven and difficult to put down, reminiscent of the great John Sayles movie *Matewan*, except told for kids.

The Tale of Desperaux by Kate DiCamillo (2003):

It's tough to choose just one of the amazingly prolific DiCamillo's books as a favorite, but this is mine. After reading and loving *Because of Winn Dixie*, I picked this one up and was blown away by this old-fashioned fairytale imbued with modern sensibilities. What emerges is an achingly raw story about good and evil that explores the territory in-between with true empathy for each character. DiCamillo is an expert at shifting genres and making them her own.

Holes
by Louis Sachar (1998):

Holes is a uniquely bizarre tale that centers around Stanley Yelnats (get it?) and is woven together with several other intersecting stories. From his "dirty-rotten-pig-stealing" great-grandfather to outlaw Kissing Kate Barlow, this complicated story really shouldn't work but, somehow, Sachar pulls it together with absolute perfection.

The Gardener
by Sarah Stewart, pictures by David Small (1997):

This book was a gift to our daughter from her grandmother, who she calls Nana. It's a Depression-era story of a family fallen on hard times and it's told with such gentle grace and tenderness through a series of letters from young Lydia Grace Finch to her family across the 10 months in which she's sent to live with her uncle in the city while her parents wait for things to get better. Accompanied by richly expressive illustrations that tell the story as much as the words, this lovely little book is a must-have in your collection.

Officer Buckle and Gloria
by Peggy Rathman, Putnam, 1995.

Later printing, signed and inscribed by the author. A truly great Caldecott winner, delightfully and compassionately written and exuberantly illustrated by the talented Rathman. Another classic in the making, if we do say so ourselves, and one of the most popular books of our little one's childhood. As good a deal as they come at **$15** in an online auction.

Image courtesy Heritage Auctions

Holes
by Louis Sachar, Farrar, Straus and Giroux, 1998.

A later printing of this popular Newberry winner, signed and inscribed by the author. A popular film also bolstered this book. At auction this copy brought **$19**.

Image courtesy Heritage Auctions

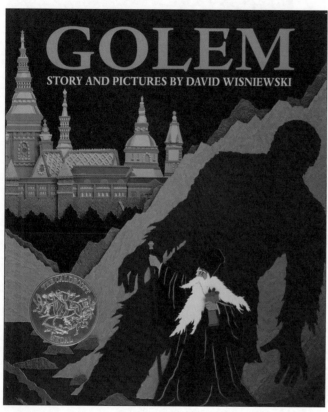

Golem
by David Wisniewski, Clarion, 1996.

Later printing of this wonderful Caldecott winner, signed and inscribed by the author. **$21**

Image courtesy Heritage Auctions

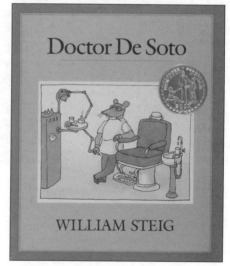

Doctor De Soto
by William Steig, Farrar, Straus and Giroux, 1983.

Second printing, signed and inscribed by the author. **$20**

Image courtesy Heritage Auctions

Animalia

by Graeme Base, Viking Kestrel, 1987.

Later printing, inscribed by the author with an original drawing, unseen here. This book, so popular in the late 1980s and early 1990s, shows that even a later edition of a book can carry value and be a treasured collectible. The owner of this book took the time and effort to get Base to sign, inscribe and draw in it, raising its value – **$53** at auction – and certainly bringing added meaning to both the original owner and the new owner.

Image courtesy Heritage Auctions

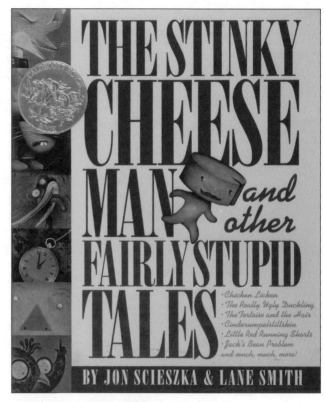

The Stinky Cheese Man

by Jon Scieszka and Lane Smith, Viking, 1992.

First Edition, first printing, signed and inscribed by both authors and with an original Stinky Cheese Man drawing. Popular with Millennials. **$50** at auction.

Image courtesy Heritage Auctions

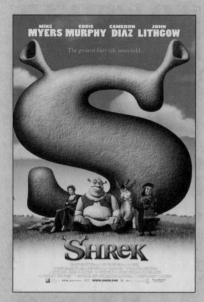

Shrek (DreamWorks, 2001) One Sheet

A pre-release movie poster for the CGI animated film version of *Shrek*, which may well have made this incredibly popular and famous kid's book even more famous and popular. The book and movie are not really the same story, but they are cut from the same cloth and the enduring popularity of both owe much to the other. This poster brought **$29** in an online auction – quite affordable for fans of the book and the movie.

Image courtesy Heritage Auctions

Shrek!

By William Steig, New York: Farrar, Straus and Giroux, 1990.

First Edition. In near fine condition this copy realized an even **$200** at auction.

Image courtesy Heritage Auctions

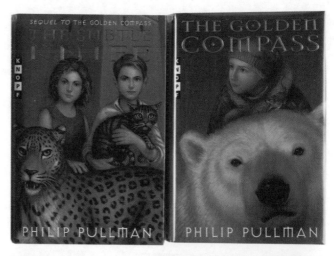

The Hunger Games Trilogy

by Suzanne Collins, New York: Scholastic Press, 2008-2010.

Titles include: *The Hunger Games; Catching Fire; Mockingjay*, all First Editions, first printings and inscribed by the author. The success of *The Hunger Games* trilogy is directly tied to the young adult series phenomenon established by Harry Potter. This inscribed set brought **$2,000** at auction. An unsigned First Edition set won't set you back that much, but, if you are buying now, it will be a few hundred. Wait a few years and see where the price settles and whether the popularity of these books is enduring.

Image courtesy Heritage Auctions

His Dark Materials Trilogy

by Phillip Pullman

Including: *The Golden Compass, The Subtle Knife* and *The Amber Spyglass*, all New York: Alfred A. Knopf, first American editions, signed by the author on the title pages. *The Amber Spyglass* is the first children's book to be awarded the Whitbread Prize and the first children's book to be nominated for the Booker Prize. This is a wonderful collection of Pullman's popular and epic trilogy. The unfortunate movie adaptation that tanked so badly in 2007 can't take the polish off these fine books or this excellent set. It ran a determined collector **$598**.

Image courtesy Heritage Auctions

J.K. ROWLING

I t's hard to call anything written in the last 20 years a true "Giant," but notice must be paid to Harry Potter – at least in the short term.

J.K. Rowling's saga of the boy-wizard Harry, the magical world that he inhabits – which runs parallel to our own, though we poor "muggles" have no idea of it – and the gathering forces of evil that it is his destiny to fight and overcome, have sold millions of copies, inspired a run of hit movies, spawned an amusement park and marketing byproducts that rival the work of Walt Disney himself. It's impressive, to say the least.

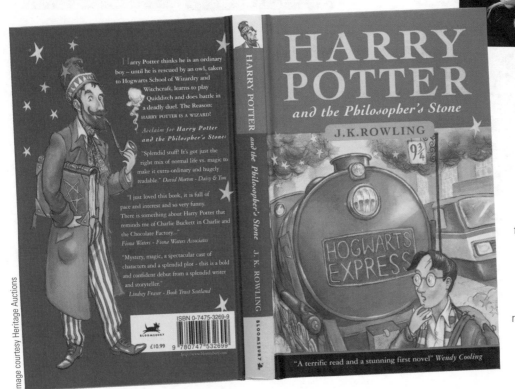

Image courtesy Heritage Auctions

Harry Potter and the Philosopher's Stone
by J. K. Rowling, London: Bloomsbury, 1997.

First Edition, first issue. Not issued with a dust jacket, this copy is now housed in a First Edition, later printing dust jacket and both are virtually new – almost unheard of for this title, which accounts for the incredible **$43,750** price. Harry Potter is obviously a touchstone for a generation of people, now working on a second generation. The original print run was very small – around 500 copies – most of which went to libraries or into the hands of children.

Complete set of Harry Potter UK Editions, all signed by author.

Complete set of all seven UK *Harry Potter* Titles Signed by J.K. Rowling, including: *Harry Potter and the Philosopher's Stone,* London: Bloomsbury, 1997, First Edition, third printing; *Harry Potter and the Chamber of Secrets*, London: Bloomsbury, 1998, First Edition, first state; *Harry Potter and the Prisoner of Azkaban*, London: Bloomsbury, 1999, First Edition; *Harry Potter and the Goblet of Fire*, London: Bloomsbury, 2000, First Edition; *Harry Potter and the Order of the Phoenix*, London: Bloomsbury, 2003, First Edition; *Harry Potter and the Half-Blood Prince*, London: Bloomsbury, 2005, First Edition; *Harry Potter and the Deathly Hallows*, London: Bloomsbury, 2007, First Edition. **$9,560**.

for Jessica, who loves stories,
for Anne, who loved them too,
and for Di, who heard this one first.

Image courtesy Heritage Auctions

Not to mention its influence on the teen fiction genre. Harry and his pals are the godparents to every vampire, werewolf, demigod and dystopian teen savior that has come down the pipe since.

Time will tell if *Harry Potter* and his friends have the staying power of the Pevensie children in *The Lion, The Witch and The Wardrobe,* or of Tolkein's *Lord of the Rings*, but the struggle of young Harry against Voldemort, the dark lord, is off to a good start. It hits the right notes along the journey and it gives us a specific and total evil to root against – there is no mistaking the good guys and the bad guys in Rowling's world.

The popularity of the books and the movies make collecting *Harry Potter* books both easy and hard. Easy because there are millions of copies out there, many of them First Editions. They are easy to find and easy to buy and will not run you much more than cover price, even less for paperbacks or later printings.

The hard side of the equation is that First Edition, first printings of any of the books are quite rare and definitely expensive, especially if we are talking about the first book, *Harry Potter and the Philosopher's Stone* – the English title on the true First Edition – because only a few hundred of these were printed, and most of them went to libraries. If you can find one, which will take some serious good luck, then you better be willing to pay into the tens of thousands of dollars.

Harry Potter and the Sorcerer's Stone (Warner Brothers, 2001) one sheet.

Featuring spectacular artwork, this poster for the first installment of the Harry Potter film series sold for **$145** at auction.

Image courtesy Heritage Auctions

The Tales of Beedle the Bard

by J. K. Rowling, London: Children's High Level Group, 2008.

Translated from the original runes by Hermione Granger. With commentary by Professor Albus Dumbledore. A deluxe collector's edition, signed by Rowling and with her official holographic sticker. **$1,250**.

Image courtesy Heritage Auctions

Original Cover Art
by Cliff Wright, ink and watercolor.

Original cover artwork (above) of *Harry Potter and the Chamber of Secrets* (right) realized **$13,750** at auction.

Image courtesy Heritage Auctions

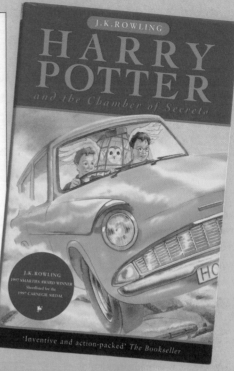

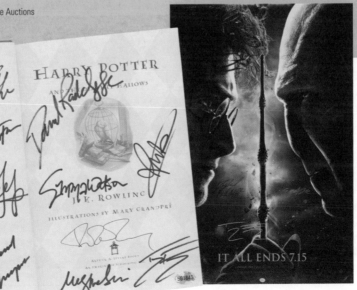

Harry Potter and The Deathly Hallows
by J.K. Rowling, Arthur L. Levine Books, 2007.

First American Edition, first printing. This book, signed by author and numerous cast members of the film by the same name, brought **$6,875** at auction. The cast-signed movie poster sold for **$13,145**.

Image courtesy Heritage Auctions

CHRIS VAN ALLSBURG

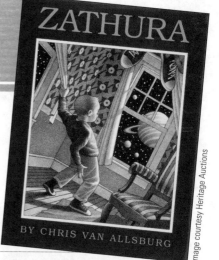

Chris Van Allsburg started out as a sculptor. He left that medium behind when he discovered his gift for illustrating and writing children's books. Born in Grand Rapids, Mich., Van Allsburg has written and illustrated

more than 20 books and has earned Caldecott Medals for *Jumanji* and *The Polar Express*. *Jumanji* was made into a movie in 1995 starring Robin Williams while *The Polar Express*, starring Tom Hanks, was a blockbuster film release in 2004. Van Allsburg's drawings are notable for their perspective, often providing a view of how a child might see the world. The bull terrier Van Allsburg includes in his books commemorates his brother-in-law's former dog.

Zathura

by Chris Van Allsburg, Boston: Houghton Mifflin, 2002.

First Edition signed by author. A fine copy of a superior book, it brought **$75** at auction and was the subject of a blink-and-you-missed-it feature film.

The Polar Express

by Chris Van Allsburg, Boston: Houghton Mifflin, 1985.

Later printing, signed and dated by the author. A very desirable book and a modern holiday classic, the Caldecott-winning book is happily un-marred by the clunky CGI film adaptation of several years ago. This copy sold at auction for **$53**.

Jumanji

by Chris Van Allsburg, Houghton Mifflin, 1981.

Later printing, signed and inscribed by the author. A book that radiates out-of-control fun with sinister monkeys and a decidedly evil board game, it remains quite popular to this day. This copy brought **$32** at auction and you should expect to pay about the same, if not a little more for a similar signed edition.

Jumanji book illustration

by Chris Van Allsburg, 1980.

Graphite on paper, 15.5 x 17 in., signed lower right. This original drawing was included in Van Allsburg's Caldecott Medal winning book, *Jumanji*, published by Houghton Mifflin Books, 1981. The owner of this piece paid a premium, **$31,070**, for Van Allsburg's superb drawing. The film version of Jumanji starred the late, great Robin Williams as a boy for years stuck in an incomplete game of the titular Jumanji.

Image courtesy Heritage Auctions

Images courtesy Heritage Auctions

FAVORITE "GLIMPSE AT THE FUTURE" BOOKS AND TRENDS

The 90-Second Newbery Film Festival

Have you heard of this? Founded by young adult writer James Kennedy in 2011, it's an annual contest in which kids create 90-second videos that tell the entire story of Newbery-winning books. Check out the best of them and the rules for entering at jameskennedy.com.

The One and Only Ivan
by Katherine Applegate (2012)

Inspired by a true story, this beautiful and haunting tale about Ivan the gorilla is told from his perspective. Our relationship to animals has changed greatly over the past 100 years. Perhaps children's stories will begin to reflect that more and the anthropomorphic characters who think and live exactly like humans will be replaced by tales such as this, where Applegate strives to create a protagonist who feels like a real gorilla.

Flora and Ulysses by Kate DiCamillo (2013)

DiCamillo is an author who adapts to different genres so easily that she has now created a whole new one! This novel of prose, combined with black and white, comic-style sequences, creates a whole new way of telling a story.

Zita the Spacegirl
by Ben Hatke (2011)

The graphic novel genre for children has expanded exponentially. In addition, girl heroes and superheroes have dramatically increased in children's literature. Hatke combines these trends in a cool space adventure that is appropriate for the younger audience. The characters are compelling and the friendships are strong. Hatke says the 3rd in the series is the last, but we're crossing our fingers for more.

The Invention of Hugo Cabret
by Brian Selznick (2007)

Selznick rocked the world of children's literature with this amazing book. A whole new way to read with both the prose and the illustrations given equal weight and equal space. The paper version of the book is preferable to a digital one. It has to be held to fully experience the art of this innovative creation.

Baby Brains by Simon James (2004)

This picture book (and the two that followed) were read over and over in our house. A fantastic story about a newborn baby so smart that he performs surgery and travels to space within the first few weeks of his life, it also pokes fun at the way modern parents strive to make their babies the best and smartest, starting in the womb. As technology grows and shapes our children, I imagine many more stories about how we raise our kids and the competitive nature of child rearing. Baby Brains cry of "I want my mommy!" is both hilarious and a reminder of what children truly need.

Moxy Maxwell Does Not Love Stuart Little by Peggy Gifford (2007)

This book is so *meta*! Our 9-year-old daughter "got it" right away and now wants to read the entire series. *Meta* is in. Expect to see this self-referential way of seeing, and expressing, the world more and more.

Oprah's Kids Book Club

Oprah changed adult reading habits when she created her Book Club. Now she has started a kid's version. Let's hope she uses her power on the right books.

Kid's National Geographic

As both magazines and nonprofit organizations struggle to stay alive National Geographic has created an empire based on kids. Its success is due to an amazing ability to adapt to the modern child. It's not just a magazine anymore, NatGeo has delved into television, the internet and a publishing company pumping out quality products that kids gobble up. Expect other publishers to follow suit.

Dystopia

Once upon a time, dystopian themes were the domain of mostly adult novels. Today this theme of a bleak future for society has overtaken young adult literature. I understand the attraction to this material for teenagers, and have to admit I haven't read much of it, as my daughter is not yet of age, but this trend concerns me. The worries of the world are with us every minute of the day in our wired society. Is this the consequence on the psyches of young people? Is this a passing fad or the new norm?

" As an adult, I would say my favorite children's books are the *Fancy Nancy* series. Love them! She's so me, with her love of all things in glorious excess. Fringe and lace and girly things. The pictures are engaging, the stories charming. I love them so much. On a gloomy, rainy Seattle afternoon, I find just looking at those books on my shelf makes the day a little brighter. **"**

SUSAN MALLERY, the New York Times best-selling author of *The Girls of Mischief Bay.*

photo by annie b/STILLS photography

Chapter 6

DISNEY

isney is, in many ways, the glue that ties all of our childhoods together. It doesn't matter what generation you were born into, Mickey Mouse, Donald Duck, Snow White, Peter Pan and every last character to flow from the genius minds of The Mouse are indelibly inked on your brain. It is no different in the realm of Children's Books.

We all read Disney books. They were the wallpaper of languid summer days, these individual adventures of Disney characters, based on the cartoons and movies that Disney was producing in convenient slim little volumes or heavy compendiums. If you have children, whether they are now 5 or 50, you will remember grabbing one off the shelf at the local library or off the rack at a store. They had no staying power, succumbing to split spines via wear and tear, or crayons lazily deployed, but they were affordable and entertaining, everything that Disney himself aspired to be.

Except that today, Disney books do indeed have staying power that is both sentimental and economical. Those that have survived – those that go back to the first Disney publishing agreements with a variety of companies in 1930 – can command great prices and even greater nostalgia.

Walt and Roy Disney, along with their first great marketing genius, Kay Kamen, saw the potential for product tie-ins all over the marketplace. Once *Steamboat Willie* hit – and after Walt had a bad experience in losing the rights to his first character, *Oswald The Lucky Rabbit* – there was little to no

way that the Disneys were going to miss the marketing boat with Mickey. The company worked with several publishers through the years, notably the David McKay Company, before and concurrent with the Western (Whitman) agreement that led to the era of Disney Little Golden Books, and produced an astonishing array of content starting in 1930 with publisher Bibo & Lang's *Mickey Mouse Book*, an extreme rarity almost never seen today.

Lucky for children, the product was good. The art was fantastic, often done by top names within the Disney fold, and the stories were familiar and easy to follow. Starting in the early 1930s with books based on already-made cartoons, Disney books populated every book, department and toy store in the country. They were affordable – especially when it came to the Golden Books – and easily accessible.

It's also important not to overlook Disney's contribution to saving a good many books from historic obscurity, some in the public domain and some not. Can you argue that P.L. Travers' *Mary Poppins* books would have survived to this day without Disney's masterful treatment of the material? Would French writer Felix Salten's obscure tale about a baby deer in the forest without a mother, titled Bambi, have been remembered at all were it not for the film? How many books that Disney made into film can we say this about? What about *Snow White and the Seven Dwarfs? Pinocchio? Peter Pan? Song of the South? Sleeping Beauty?* The list goes on and on, to the

point that the popular visual record of many of these books is based completely on the film adaptations, no matter how great the original art work may have been.

There is almost no area of 20th century American (Western) culture that Walt Disney and the Disney Company did not touch, an influence that has shown no sign of slowing as the 21st century has dawned. Such was, and is, the remarkable power of The Mouse. We know, objectively, through auction records that early Disney remains collectible in all segments, with none stronger than books – a good sign for anyone out there contemplating starting or bolstering a collection. It is within these books, too – more than any other Disney collectible – that the history of the Disney juggernaut can be told.

While no one name, title or publisher can claim to be the backbone of the entire niche of collectible children's books, Disney can certainly make a case for being the most consistent and steady workhorse children's books have. From old to new, across all eras, the output was consistently strong and consistently entertaining. This adds up to an authoritative presence wherever you look and whatever you collect. Open your eyes and take a good look around, wherever you search. We can guarantee there is some kind of Disney treasure within arm's reach.

Lady and the Tramp

by Ward Greene (Walt Disney Studios), New York: Simon and Schuster, 1953.

First Edition. **$200** in an online auction.

Image courtesy Heritage Auctions

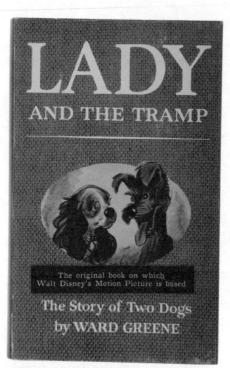

Walt Disney's Story of Mickey Mouse

1932, First Edition, first printing. **$47** online.

Image courtesy Heritage Auctions

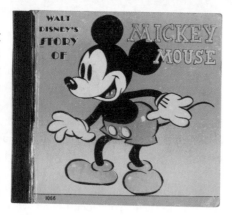

The Story of Mickey Mouse and the Smugglers

Walt Disney, Racine, WI: Whitman Publishing, 1935.

No telling if Walt really wrote this book — we suspect not. More than likely it was based on a cartoon or an idea Walt had for a cartoon and, since he was *Walt Disney* after all, and it was 1935, the credit goes to him. **$131** at auction.

Image courtesy Heritage Auctions

A Pair of Mickey Mouse Story Books

Including: *Mickey Mouse in Pigmy Land*, London and Glasgow: Collins Clear-Type Press, no date, First Edition – a beautiful copy that has miraculously escaped the ravages of time – and *Mickey Mouse Bedtime Stories*, London and Glasgow: The Sunshine Press, no date, First Edition. These sold together at auction for just under **$120**.

Image courtesy Heritage Auctions

Mickey Mouse and the Magic Carpet
Walt Disney Enterprises, New York: Kay Kamen, 1935.

First Edition. Expect to pay **$125** or more for a good copy of this book. It is interesting to note the publishing credit to Kay Kamen, the first licensing partner Disney had and, arguably, the man who established the template for the global marketing supremacy Disney has perfected.

Image courtesy Heritage Auctions

Mickey Mouse and Friends #904
Linen-like Story Book, Whitman, 1936

Attractive and colorful 12-page children's storybook. **$227** in an online auction.

Image courtesy Heritage Auctions

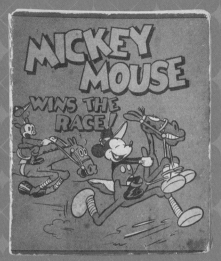
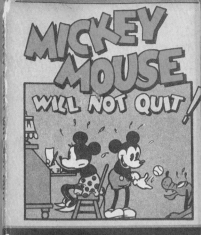
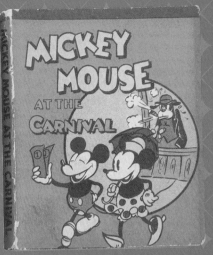
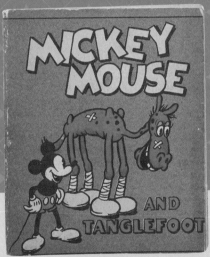
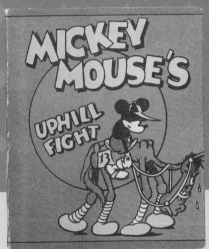
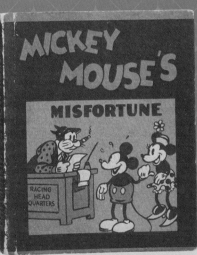

Walt Disney, lot of six Mickey Mouse Miniature Books

All volumes Racine, WI: Whitman Publishing Company, 1934

Includes *Mickey Mouse and Tanglefoot*, *Mickey Mouse Will Not Quit*, *Mickey Mouse's Uphill Fight*, *Mickey Mouse Wins the Race*, *Mickey Mouse's Misfortune*, and *Mickey Mouse at the Carnival*. A wonderful little early Disney grouping like this would set you back about **$180**, but be well worth it.

Image courtesy Heritage Auctions

MOVIES/TV SHOWS BASED ON KIDS' BOOKS

The Wizard of Oz (1939):

L. Frank Baum may have written the greatest American fairytale, but Hollywood made it a classic, an institution and an influence around the world. At this point, many don't even know it was a book first. The movie's appeal lies, of course, in the spectacular production details, but the storytelling keeps us coming back, rooted as it is in the deepest of human themes: *There's No Place Like Home*. From *Star Wars* to *Lost*, *Wizard* keeps coming up and probably always will.

Willy Wonka and the Chocolate Factory (1971):

Gene Wilder was clearly born to play Willy Wonka and he carries this oddly constructed, low budget film adaptation. This first version captures the essence of the strange and delicious magic that makes the book such a beloved classic.

Dr. Seuss' How The Grinch Stole Christmas TV Special (1966):

This classic Chuck Jones animated special is, in my opinion, one of the best book to television adaptations ever. The animation, Boris Karloff's voice, the music... all of it does justice to one of the greatest Christmas stories ever told by Dr. Seuss, a legend of children's literature.

Babe (1983):

A film that honors author Dick King-Smiths' masterwork. This is a quirky, smart little film, with a light touch, about individualism and conformity. Filmed to look like a storybook, Babe is a plucky pig with child-like awakenings to the realities of the world. The story, told in a seamless blend of real animals and CGI, comes to life when the Farmer dances a jig for sickly Babe. It's a special moment between animal and human rarely seen on film. In fact, actor James Cromwell, who plays the Farmer, became vegetarian after making the film!

Curious George PBS Kids Show (2006 to present):

Not wanting to leave my toddler alone in front of the TV, I was so relieved and thankful to find this cartoon – a kid's show I sincerely enjoyed watching. The animators perform a miracle, modernizing George and all his friends without losing the essence of this classic series of books by H.A. and Margret Rey. In fact, they took this gem of a story and made it even better. Smart, funny and full of lessons on math, science and life. It even has a theme song by Dr. John.

Winnie-the-Pooh (2011):

Although I was a big fan of the old Disney Pooh featurettes (1966, 1968 and 1974), they didn't hold up when I showed them to my daughter. In a rare instance, I prefer Disney's modern version, which took it to a new level. The dedication is apparent in the "old-fashioned" hand animation and we all enjoyed the cartoon short beforehand. The detailed plot points come right from the book and tell a simple, sweet story that is perfect for younger children. At barely more than an hour, it never lags or gets boring and the few musical numbers are enjoyable. A rare treat in this world of over-the-top special effects layered on weak stories.

Shrek (2001):

The book turned the fairy tale on its head, questioning the concepts of good and evil, beauty and ugliness, and forever influencing children's books. The same can be said for the film. Shrek the movie is a visual delight. It's a jolly and wicked adaptation filled with puns, jokes and pop culture references that forever changed movies for children. Hollywood made the story more palatable but the film retains the essence of William Steig's original work.

Mary Poppins (1964):

So it's old-fashioned, a bit dated and more saccharine than the book – just what author P. L. Travers was afraid of – yet this film is a complete joy and pure magic. The music by The Sherman Brothers is spectacular and the innovative use of animation remains stunning. Most of all, it's a pleasure to show to children. No fast cuts, no 3-D, no over-the-top CGI. Just the lovely story of a fracturing family and the nanny who helps them reconnect and remember what's important.

Old Yeller (1957):

It's a sentimental tearjerker, it's dated, features unfavorable stereotypes, lots of guns and realistic animal fights – PETA wasn't around back then – yet this film has become part of our culture. Find anyone who's seen it and dare them to deny they cried when Old Yeller dies. The success of this movie convinced Disney to devote more time to live action pictures in the late 1950s and early 1960s. This film is out of bounds for the faint-hearted and children under 10.

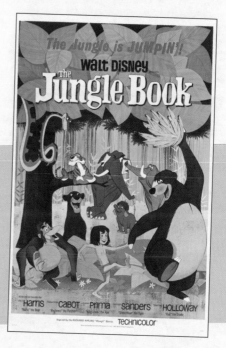

The Jungle Book (1967):

The last Disney film to have Walt's magic touch; he died during the making. Very loosely based on the Mowgli stories from Rudyard Kipling's book, what emerges is something different, but wonderful. Everyone involved with the film was at the peak of their talents, even though it's not considered a classic on the order of *Snow White* or *Cinderella*. A perfectly lively, funny adventure story that still captivates. I confess to know all the song lyrics by heart - The Sherman Brothers rock!

Walt Disney Studios, *Walt Disney's Fantasia*
by Deems Taylor, New York, 1940.

First Edition. **$688** at auction.

Image courtesy Heritage Auctions

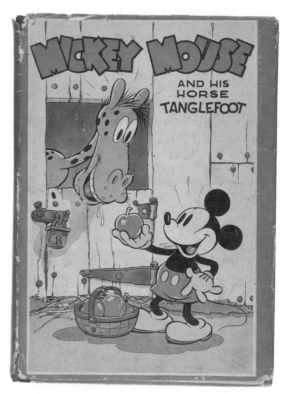

Walt Disney Studios, *Mickey Mouse and His Horse Tanglefoot*
Philadelphia: David McKay Company, 1936.

First Edition, with numerous color illustrations in text illustrated by the staff of Walt Disney Studios. A very good copy like this, in the seldom seen original dust jacket, would run in the range of **$1,100** at auction; lesser copies, lesser prices, though the enjoyment of seeing this on your bookshelf in any state would be considerable.

Image courtesy Heritage Auctions

Walt Disney Studios, *The "Pop-Up" Silly Symphonies Containing Babes in the Woods and King Neptune*

New York: Blue Ribbon Books, Inc., 1933.

First Edition, with 34 illustrations including four double-page pop ups illustrated by the staff of Walt Disney Studios. A beautiful copy of this desirable Disney pop-up, it brought **$938**, at the higher end of the spectrum for Disney ephemera, but well worth it considering a) it's not a Mickey book and b) it's based on the *Silly Symphonies* cartoons, which were Walt's first great success, preceding even that of his beloved little mouse.

Image courtesy Heritage Auctions

Walt Disney Studios, *Mickey Mouse Waddle Book*

New York: Blue Ribbon Books, 1934.

First Edition. An amazingly clean, complete, bright set and one of the rarest of any Disney book, waddle books were immensely popular at the dawn of the Disney empire and these things sold by the thousands to eager kids who couldn't wait to punch out the waddles and have a good time with the famous, mischievous mouse. Disney was a juggernaut in animation and in marketing and these waddle books, so popular in their day, remain equally popular today, though that popularity is about their elusiveness rather than their availability. If you see one, intact, grab it and don't look back. This one went for **$3,750**, a good price for the rarity!

Image courtesy Heritage Auctions

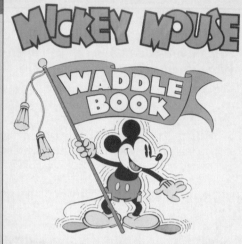

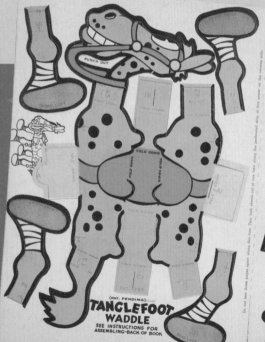

Snow White and the Seven Dwarfs

Half sheet, style A movie poster (RKO, 1937).

A Holy Grail piece for Disney lovers, this is a copy of the incredibly elusive Style A half sheet movie poster, with artwork by legendary children's book/animator Gustaf Tenggren. It is Tenggren's work (out of some 570 artists that worked on the film) that distinguishes many of the film's finest moments, as seen here in this simply splendid illustration of Snow White fleeing the murderous huntsman. **$4,481** at auction.

Image courtesy Heritage Auctions

Gustaf Tenggren
(American, 1896-1970)

Snow White and the Seven Dwarfs, original promotional art, 1937.

Mixed media on paper. The coming of Walt Disney's first feature-length animated film shook the world of animation with its innovation and resulted in this wonderfully detailed movie poster illustration by the great children's book artist Gustaf Tenggren. In 1936 Tenggren was hired by The Walt Disney Company to work as the stylist on *Snow White and the Seven Dwarfs,* the first American feature-length animated film. He created the distinctive, Old World look that Walt Disney sought. Tenggren's drawing captures perfectly the major characteristics of each of the Dwarfs, as well as the resonant, timeless beauty of Snow White. This was the original art used as the centerpiece of the Snow White movie poster, a rarity in and of itself. **$59,750**.

Image courtesy Heritage Auctions

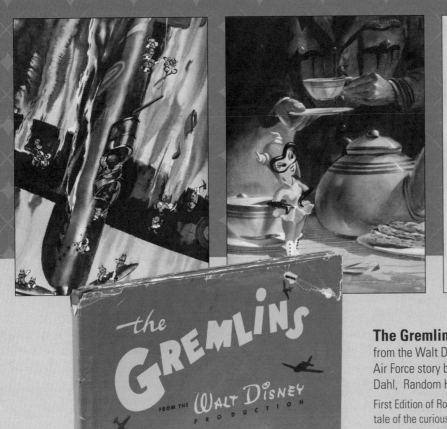

The Gremlins

from the Walt Disney Production, a Royal Air Force story by Flight Lieutenant Roald Dahl, Random House, New York, 1934.

First Edition of Roald Dahl's first book, a fanciful tale of the curious little creatures, driven from their homes in the trees by the march of wartime industries, that plagued aviators imaginations. Despite Dahl's British nationality, this was first published in the U.S., intended to accompany a Disney animated film that was never produced. **$540** at auction.

Images courtesy Justin Benttinen/PBA Galleries

The Adventures of Mickey Mouse – Book 1
by Walt Disney, David McKay, Philadelphia, 1931.

First Edition and a nice copy of the first Disney-published Mickey Mouse book. Scarce in jacket. Estimate **$1,000+**.

Images courtesy Justin Benttinen/PBA Galleries

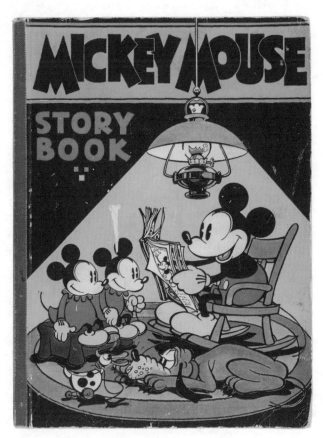

Mickey Mouse Story Book

by Walt Disney, David McKay, Philadelphia, 1931.

Story and illustrations by staff of Walt Disney studio. This is a very early appearance of Mickey Mouse, the most recognized cartoon character in the world, at the naissance of his popularity. **$120** at auction.

Image courtesy Justin Benttinen/PBA Galleries

Walt Disney's Thumper

by Walt Disney, Grosset & Dunlap, New York, 1942.

First Edition, illustrations in color and black & white. Based on the character created by Walt Disney for the motion picture "Bambi," which took Disney Studios years to make and was not near as beloved at its release as it became with subsequent releases and generations. **$96**.

Image courtesy of Justin Benttinen/PBA Galleries

Walt Disney's Donald Duck

by Walt Disney, Whitman Publishing Co., Racine, WI, 1935.

First Edition, illustrations by the staff of the Walt Disney Studios. An historic volume for the first appearance of Donald Duck, here featured along with the nephews of Mickey Mouse. **$330**

Images courtesy Justin Benttinen/PBA Galleries

"Is the water deep?" Donald asked. "It's over your head!" the two nephews answered. "Okay, then," Donald exclaimed. "Here's a dive such as you've never seen before! Ready? One - TWO - THREE!"

With a big spring, Donald bounced high into the air. Then down he came, head first, his nose pointing right for the water and the splash. But instead of a splash there was a SCRUNCH!

Bambi (RKO, 1942)
Six sheet movie poster

This eye-popping six sheet is by far the best paper on Disney's legendary revolutionary multi-plane Technicolor feature based on the Felix Salter book, originally written in French. This is one of the most rare Disney posters and is much nicer than most of the posters from this original release. **$3,107**

Image courtesy Heritage Auctions

Al White (American 20th Century), Walt Disney's Mary Poppins, Little Golden Book cover illustration, 1964

Gouache on board with an acetate and acrylic paint overlay, 16 x 13in. Not signed. **$567** at auction.

Image courtesy Heritage Auctions

Pinocchio (Buena Vista, R-1971)
One Sheet movie poster

Starring the voices of Dick Jones, Cliff Edwards, Walter Catlett, Evelyn Venable and Christian Rub, this poster is from a 1972 re-release of the film, demonstrating the staying power of Disney – the film is still watched and venerated and the original children's book, if respected, is not read even 1/100th as much as the film is viewed. **$62**.

Image courtesy Heritage Auctions

Cinderella (RKO, 1950) One Sheet

The slipper-less Cinderella and her handsome prince are still the quintessential fairytale images, as seen on this color-rich one sheet from Disney's timeless tale. The **$777** price may seem steep, but that's the power of the Disney magic!

Image courtesy Heritage Auctions

Peter Pan and the Darling Family Production Cel and Master Background
Walt Disney, 1953.

This production cel of George and Mary Darling, Wendy, and Nana standing at the window of their home is placed over a hand-painted Key Master background of the Darling residence. Added to this setup is a perfect production cel of Peter Pan in flight. A stunningly beautiful setup demonstrating the breadth of Disney's vision, which only added to the sparkle that already surrounded the beloved tale. **$8,963** at auction.

Image courtesy Heritage Auctions

Peter Pan (RKO, 1953) One Sheet movie poster

If you still believe in childlike wonderment, adventure, and that growing up is overrated, this delightful one sheet featuring Peter Pan and the gang is the one for you. After almost two decades of production, Walt Disney's vision of J. M. Barrie's Peter Pan finally hit movie screens in 1953 and met with resounding success. The story of the perpetual boy, Peter, and his escapades in Neverland, his encounters with the Darling family, and of course, the villainous Captain Hook, are beautifully rendered by Disney's famed "Nine Old Men," the animators who were responsible for the distinctive Disney animation style. **$2,868** at auction for such a fine copy.

Image courtesy Heritage Auctions

GARTH WILLIAMS
THE GOLD STANDARD

Within the history of Children's Books there are a handful of illustrators who leave a mark that is so indelible that the names of the books they illustrated and the art they created for those books are completely inseparable.

Garth Montgomery Williams (American, 1912-1996) was such an illustrator. So much so, in fact, that we would argue that he is perhaps the greatest and most versatile illustrator of the 20th century. Williams was not a writer, first and foremost – though he did author six books, including the very famous and controversial *The Rabbit's Wedding* – he was an artist. His classification is outside of other children's books creators, because Williams was a genius who mostly gave his talents to other author's titles, hence the unbelievable diversity in his more than 60 illustrated works.

Williams is known today, primarily, for three titles: *Charlotte's Web* by E.B. White, *Stuart Little* by E.B. White and *Little House on the Prairie* by Laura Ingalls Wilder, though he also illustrated the rest of the series. It's ridiculous, however,

to stop there as regards to his work. His free-flowing, musical style, so jazzy and compelling, provided a through line to all of his work, whether he was drawing dogs, cats, bunnies, pigs, mice, kittens, elves, fairies or adults. As Mel Gussow of the *New York Times* put it in his May 10, 1996 obituary of Williams, "Although the books were written by a diverse range of authors, the drawings all had Mr. Williams impeccable, heartwarming touch."

We can't think of a better way to say it.

Of *Charlotte's Web,* the best-selling children's book of all time, is there a way to think of the book outside Williams' depiction of Wilbur the pig, Charlotte the spider and Fern, the young girl? No.

Stuart Little? Impossible not to see Williams' dapper little mouse in association with the title. Impossible.

Little House on the Prairie? While Williams was not the illustrator of the books when they were first released in the 1930s (Helen Sewell had that honor), Williams' 1950s illustrations of the Ingalls family and the hardships they face are, without a doubt, the definitive versions. As Harper editor Ursula Nordstrom, who gave Williams his first break on *Stuart Little*, wrote, Williams – New York-born to British artist parents, and raised in England – "had no roots in any part of the Wilder country. But as we know, thought-kin is closer than blood-kin, and Garth certainly had all the emotional equipment, as well as the technical, to illustrate these wonderful family books."

These three stand out, with history judging both the books and the art well, but the rest of the Williams oeuvre is equally dense with great examples. Williams did some of his finest work on George Selden's wonderful Tucker Mouse, Harry Cat and Chester Cricket series that began with the sublime *The Cricket in Times Square*. He was a frequent collaborator with the legendary Margaret Wise Brown (seven books, including *Little Fur Family, The Sailor Dog and Home for a Bunny*). Williams masterfully illustrated all four volumes of Margery Sharp's *The Rescuers* series and he created amazing visuals for a host of other writers, including Russell Hoban, Else Minarik, Charlotte Zolotow and Dorothy Kunhardt.

Books that bear Williams' art are both very collectible and very readable, whichever you prefer. In the fall of 2010, Williams' estate released his art archive for sale via Heritage Auctions, which included many of the original drawings for his most beloved art, and the response was immediate and massive from collectors – with select pieces, several of which follow this introduction, selling for high five figure prices and, in some cases, into six figures – and a secondary market in Williams work, one that dealt with him purely as an author and on his own terms, was born. If you're interested in these as a collector or a fan, they are not hard to find online.

Keep a keen eye out for Williams' work the next time you are in a bookstore, browsing online or checking out an auction. In short order you'll begin to notice that not only does his work seem to be everywhere, but, simply, that it's *just that good.*

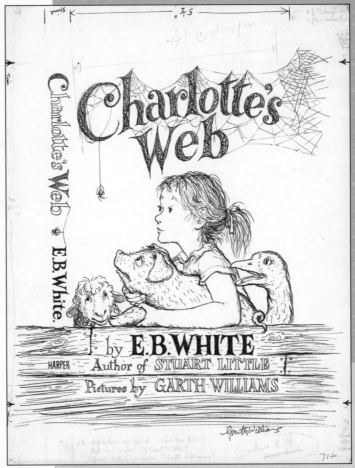

Garth Williams' original *Charlotte's Web* book cover from 1952.

This graphite and ink on paper, 14 x 11 in. work is signed by Williams in the lower right corner. It's impossible to think of this book – among the dozens that Williams did – without directly associating it with this artwork. The work sold a few years ago at auction for **$155,350**. We would venture a guess this would bring significantly more were it to cross the block again today. From the Estate of Garth Williams.

Image courtesy Heritage Auctions

Garth Williams, original pencil art and color separation/ layout materials for cover art of *Little House in the Big Woods* by Laura Ingalls Wilder, 1953.

This was the art used for the later Harper Crest Library edition. From the Estate of Garth Williams. **$3,500**

Image courtesy Heritage Auctions

Garth Williams, *On the Banks of Plum Creek* (The Little House Series) original cover art.

Watercolor on paper, signed lower right. From the Estate of Garth Williams. **$16,250**.

Image courtesy Heritage Auctions

Garth Williams, original drawing for the Laura Ingalls Wilder Award, 1954.

Original circular drawing featuring Laura Ingalls Wilder as a child, holding a doll, signed "Garth" on the front with full signature on the reverse with instructions to return the drawing to him in Aspen, Colorado. The Wilder Award is a bronze medal awarded to an author or artist by the Association for Library Service to Children, a division of the American Library Association, for excellence in children's literature. From the Estate of Garth Williams. **$2,750**

Garth Williams, *Little House on the Prairie*, original cover art, 1953

Pencil on tracing paper, signed lower right. From the Estate of Garth Williams. **$50,788**

Garth Williams, *Little Fur Family*, group of four.

page 8, 18, 22, and 25 illustrations, 1946: Pen, watercolor, and gouache on board, not signed. From the Estate of Garth Williams. **$15,000**

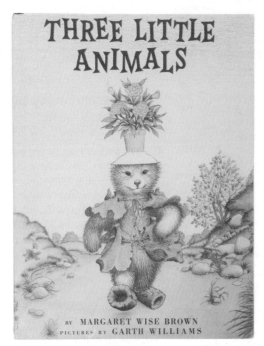

Three Little Animals
by Margaret Wise Brown, pictures by Garth Williams, New York: Harper and Brothers, 1956.

First Edition. **$62** online

Image courtesy Heritage Auctions

Large lot of Garth Williams' 70 original preliminary rough sketches for *Adventures of Benjamin Pink*, circa 1951.

In varying sizes, all either signed or initialed by Williams. A steal at auction for **$1,875**. What would you pay for the sketches of an absolute master? We imagine it would be more than this. As the years wind on and Williams' stature grows, there will come a day when his fans shake their heads in wonder at paying so little for so much from one of the all-time greats.

Image courtesy Heritage Auctions

MY FAVORITES: SERIES

The Blossom Family books
by Betsy Byars (1986-1991):

"Faulkner for kids." That's what my husband and I call this series of five books starting with "The Not-Just-Anybody Family." The Blossoms are still reeling from the bull riding death of their dad, and what follows is a wild, hilarious and heartwarming tale about what it means to be part of a family. Singular, vivid characters — mom Vicki, kids Junior, Maggie and Vern, granddad Pap with his faithful dog Mud — we become completely involved with. Byars' story is of a family like no other, yet we see ourselves in each of them.

Sophie by Dick King-Smith (1988-1995):

While reading all of Dick King-Smith's books, we discovered this gem of a series about a stubborn, opinionated girl whose life ambition is to become a "Lady Farmer." King-Smith gives us a real portrait of the English countryside — including accents and dialect — as we watch Sophie grow, from age 4 to 7. You can't help but root for her with her loveable temper, her disheveled appearance, her funny sayings and the remarkable clarity of her ambition.

Mr. Putter and Tabby
by Cynthia Rylant (1994-present):

When I returned to children's books in the library after my daughter's birth, Cynthia Rylant reassured me that good children's books were alive and well. Of her many wonderful works, I was always particularly fond of old Mr. Putter and his companionable cat Tabby. Rylant's ability to make the elderly Mr. Putter relatable to kids is astonishing. He's mischievous, child-like and a lover of snacks. The loveable cast, the vibrant illustrations and the hilarious situations make these books a must.

Calvin Coconut
by Graham Salisbury (2009 to present):

A refreshing, upbeat series about a boy who manages to be both cool and funny but also bighearted. Making the the series even better, Calvin happens to be growing up on the island of Oahu, Hawaii, as did the author. The familiarity shows in Salisbury's portrayal of the locals. It's a contemporary family dynamic and the dialog is both fun and realistic.

Brambley Hedge
by Jill Barklem (1980 to 2010):

The detailed illustrations in these books about the mice of Brambley Hedge beg to be pored over again and again. Barklem has created a self-sufficient, well-organized community and makes them come to life in these sweet little stories. We're ready to pack up and move to Brambley Hedge.

Winnie-the-Pooh series
by A.A. Milne (1924-1928):

If I had to choose one selection from children's literature to bring on a desert island, it would be this series. Milne knew how to write for children like no other while also packing wisdom, poetry and musings on adulthood into these simple tales about Christopher Robin and his animal friends living in the Enchanted Forest. Want to be *more* in awe of Milne's work? Pick up Benjamin Hoff's *The Tao of Pooh* (1982) and *The Te of Piglet* (1992).

Frances the Badger series
by Russell Hoban (1960-1972):

We still repeat many of the songs in our house that Frances makes up to deal with the tribulations of growing up. Hoban, clearly an experienced father, covers topics relevant to all families of young children – bedtime avoidance, picky eating, bullies – in a wonderfully compassionate fashion. Frances' family is always comforting and she always finds her way. Wonderful illustrations (first book by Garth Williams, the rest by wife Lillian Hoban) make Frances and her family come alive.

Garth Williams' preliminary drawings for illustrations featured in *Bedtime for Frances* written by Russell Hoban, 1960.

Image courtesy Heritage Auctions

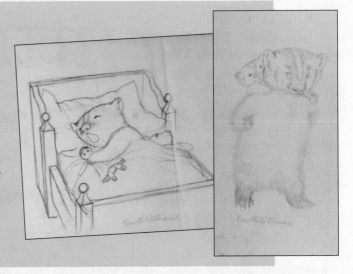

Little House on the Prairie
by Laura Ingalls Wilder, then others (1932-Present):

This series remains an invaluable contribution to American children's literature. Depicting frontier life for American pioneers in the late-1800s, they are historical fiction for children at its best. Learning about the daily life of families long ago is fascinating, and the more advanced society becomes, the more this type of story becomes important. The way the family churned butter, tapped maple trees and built or crafted almost everything they needed enthralled me as a child.

The Chronicles of Narnia
by C.S. Lewis (1950-1956):

This is the original fantasy series for children and one of the finest. Lewis weaves a rich tale about the magical world of Narnia into these seven books. He goes deep using religious allegory, mythology and fairy tales to tell an epic adventure with compelling characters. Encouraging for the mind, inspiring for the heart.

Diary of a Worm
by Doreen Cronin (2003-2007):

These three books (including *Diary of a Spider* and *Diary of a Fly*) are written in a diary format (accompanied by Harry Bliss' full-color, cartoon style illustrations) in which kids will love seeing insects in familiar settings – school, playground, home – playing with friends and doing chores. Laugh-out-loud funny with a great message: we could all get along if we just got to know one another. Cronin has a smart sense of humor, imbues her characters with hilarious personalities and is never preachy.

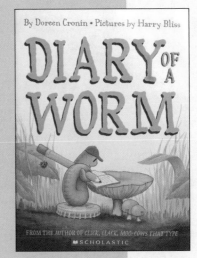

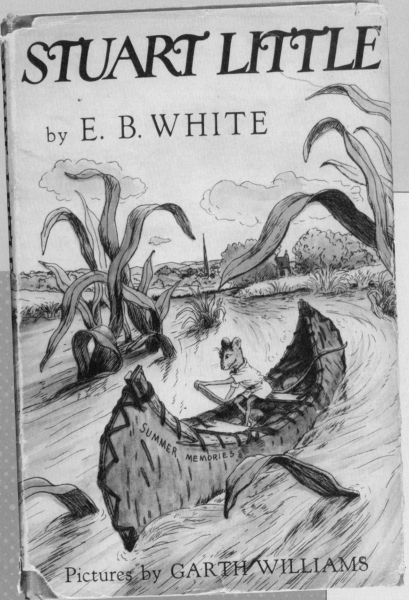

Stuart Little
by E.B. White, New York: Harper & Brothers, 1945.

First Edition, first printing, inscribed by White on the half-title page, "For Max / from E B White." Illustrated by Garth Williams and signed by him in pencil on the lower margin of the frontispiece. **$3,500**

Image courtesy Heritage Auctions

**Garth Williams, *Stuart Little,
The Arrival of Stuart Little*,
page 1 illustration, 1945.**

Ink on paper laid on board, signed lower right.
"When Mrs. Frederick C. Little's second son
arrived, everybody noticed that he was not
much bigger than a mouse. The truth of the
matter was, the baby looked very much like
a mouse in every way." From the Estate of
Garth Williams. **$65,725**

Image courtesy Heritage Auctions

Garth Williams, *The Cricket in Times Square*, original cover art, 1960.

Watercolor, gouache, and ink on paper, signed lower left. There are not enough words to describe how much we, and our daughter, love this book. Partly it is from Selden's gorgeous prose, but it may be more so because of Williams' frenetic, musical drawings that so perfectly capture the characters and the settings. From the Estate of Garth Williams. **$15,535**

Image courtesy Heritage Auctions

Garth Williams, *Do You Know What I'll Do?*, frontispiece illustration, 1958.

Pen and watercolor on board, signed. From the Estate of Garth Williams. From a group of eight that sold for **$2,375**.

Image courtesy Heritage Auctions

Garth Williams,
***Wait Till the
Moon Is Full,***
**rear flyleaf
illustration, 1948.**

Watercolor on board,
signed upper right.
From the Estate of Garth
Williams. **$5,156**

Image courtesy Heritage Auctions

**Flossie and Bossie,
original cover art, 1949.**

Pen and watercolor on paper laid on cardstock, signed by Williams *From* the Estate of Garth Williams. **$4,063**

Image courtesy Heritage Auctions

**The Tall Book of
Make-Believe,
cover illustration, 1950.**

Pencil and watercolor on paper, not signed. From the Estate of Garth Williams. **$2,500**.

Image courtesy Heritage Auctions

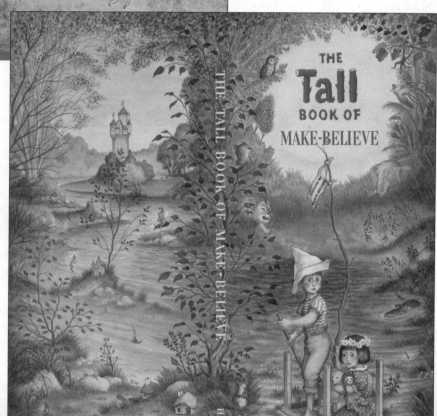

Illustrations from *The Adventures of Benjamin Pink*, group of six, 1951.

Page 86, 87, 88, 90, 96 and 105 illustrations. Pencil on tracing paper, all signed. From the Estate of Garth Williams. **$2,750** (for all six).

Image courtesy Heritage Auctions

Garth Williams, *Robin Hood*, original book illustrations, 1948

Pen on paper, all signed. *From the Estate of Garth Williams.* Illustration part of a group of 20 that sold for **$2,875**.

Image courtesy Heritage Auctions

***Emmett's Pig*, original cover art.**

Pen and ink wash on board, not signed. From the Estate of Garth Williams. **$2,375**.

Image courtesy Heritage Auctions

Watercolor Illustration of Goldilocks for
***Three Bedtime Stories*, c. 1958.**

Signed by the artist. From the Estate of Garth Williams. **$1,125**.

Image courtesy Heritage Auctions

***The Happy Orpheline*, original cover art, 1957.**

Pen and ink wash on board, signed. From the Estate of Garth Williams. **$1,375** online.

Image courtesy Heritage Auctions

The Rabbits' Wedding, I Wish You Were All Mine, page 22 and 23 illustrations, 1958.

Ink wash, pencil, and charcoal on board, signed lower right. From the Estate of Garth Williams. *"The little black rabbit opened his eyes very wide and thought very hard. 'I wish you were all mine!' said the little black rabbit."* **$8,963**

Image courtesy Heritage Auctions

The Rabbits' Wedding, original cover art, 1958.

Ink wash, pencil, and charcoal on board, signed lower right. This book was incredibly controversial in its day, due to the fact that it is about a White Bunny and Black Bunny who decide to marry. Rather than see it as the simple tale of love and devotion that Williams intended, many in the late 1950s saw it as a subversive message of integration and racial harmony. From our perch more than a half-century later this seems rather foolish, but this warm and fuzzy book was a hot potato in its day. From the Estate of Garth Williams. **$17,925**.

Image courtesy Heritage Auctions

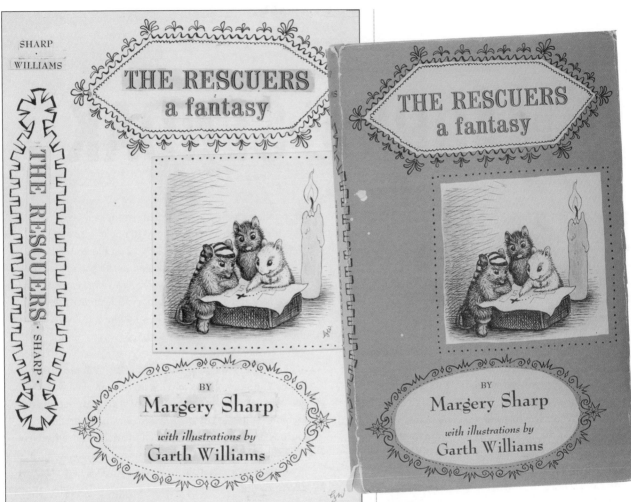

**The Rescuers,
original cover art, 1959.**

Pen and ink on board, initialed lower right.
From the Estate of Garth Williams. **$6,875**

Image courtesy Heritage Auctions

The Rescuers

by Margery Sharp, Garth Williams,
illustrator, Little, Brown, 1959.

First Edition, first printing. Very well priced
at **$47** at auction. An amazing book!

Image courtesy Heritage Auctions

Chapter 8

MAURICE SENDAK

If Maurice Sendak had done nothing in his life but give us *Where the Wild Things Are*, we would all agree that his was an exceptional contribution. The sublime artwork, the taut narrative, the ability to speak directly to children in a visual language that has entranced 50 years of readers. *Wild Things* is the standard by which all others are judged. End of story.

Maurice Sendak, however, was much more than *Wild Things*. He was a juggernaut, a philosopher, a teacher and an endless champion of books. What is there not to love about the man? He won the Caldecott, the Hans Christian Andersen Award for Illustration, the Laura Ingalls Wilder Award and the National Medal of the Arts, given by President Clinton in 1996. He wrote and illustrated more than 20 books and was the illustrator, in some form or another, on more than 90 others. Prolific just doesn't begin to cover his incredible influence.

We lost Sendak in 2012 at the age of 83, but the richness of his legacy cannot be overstated. Sendak possessed an uncanny ability to cut right to the heart of childhood – the irrational exuberance, the overbearing melancholy, the unbidden dread and fear always a breath away. Children responded to all of these things in Sendak's self-taught style and he responded right back with unimpeachable honesty in all of his work. What emerges is a great artist, not just a creator of children's books. Sendak is transcendent of genre in the public estimation. He is a giant among giants.

With his name on more than 110 books – 22 of which were named to the *New York Times* Best Illustrated Books of the Year list – he is most famous for a trilogy and a quartet: *Where The Wild Things Are, In The Night Kitchen* and *Outside Over There* and *The Nutshell Library: Alligators All Around, Chicken Soup With Rice, One Was Johnny* and *Pierre*. Within these seven works you really do have everything you need to know about Sendak.

Where The Wild Things Are is now the quintessential classic, the story of Max and the night he misbehaves, gets sent to his room (without supper) and sets out on an incredible odyssey; *In The Night Kitchen* is the dreamy journey of young Mickey through the richly evocative New York City of Sendak's childhood, the movies and comic books he so adored as a child, as well as a few cakes; *Outside Over There*, in which Ida must rescue her baby sister, who has been captured by goblins, may be the most sublime and terrifying of them all, as well as the most quietly brilliant and gorgeous.

In *The Nutshell Library*, published in 1962 – pre-*Wild Things* – you have Sendak at his simple best, with wonderful rhymes, maddening main characters and, always, unexpected outcomes. *Pierre* gets what he deserves, *Alligators All Around* will make you view the alphabet in a whole new way, *Chicken Soup With Rice* is a wonderful homage to that magic elixir

Image courtesy Heritage Auctions

This magnificent Sendak original *Wild Things* backdrop landscape, ink and watercolor on paper, brought **$74,688** at auction a few years ago. It would bring a good deal more today if it were on the block. To say that original *Wild Things*-related art is rare is an extreme understatement, and this piece is magnificent. Sendak donated much of his original work to various institutions and his estate also holds a good bit.

known as Jewish Penicillin, and Johnny eventually gets things settled down – and gets back to his book – in *One Was Johnny*.

From a collecting standpoint, Sendak is always a good bet and always welcome on bookshelves. There's never a shortage to be had at auction, or online. You'll pay anywhere from a few dollars up to several thousand, depending on the edition, so keep an open mind and heed the examples that follow. Prices have not necessarily gone up overall on Sendak's work since his death, though original signed and/or inscribed editions are bound to bring a premium above unsigned copies.

As far as Sendak original art goes, there is simply not that much of it out there – Sendak had his art carefully archived and kept, and he donated and loaned much if it to various institutions – but what there is will bring a premium. Very little has shown up in the few years since his death, so the prices that are reflected in the following pages would likely be a decent bit higher today were they to show up on the auction block. A word of advice: if you see any Sendak art, and you can afford it, *buy it. Immediately.*

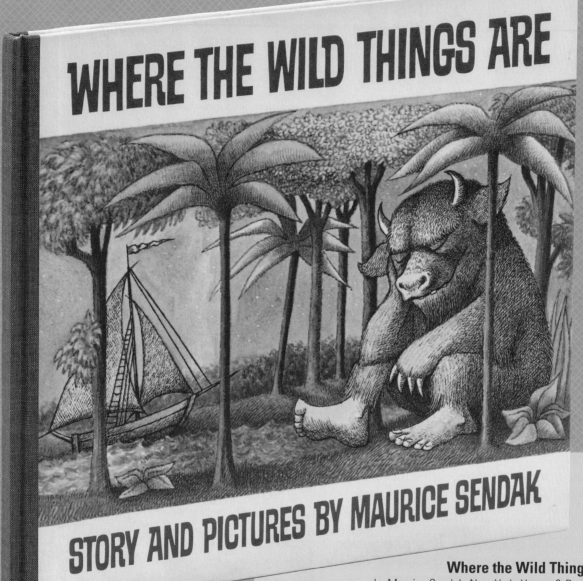

Where the Wild Things Are

by Maurice Sendak, New York: Harper & Row, 1963.

First Edition, first issue dust jacket with $3.50 price intact and no mention of the Caldecott Award on the jacket flaps, nor with the metallic medal sticker on the front of the jacket. This beauty of a copy sold for **$8,400** at auction.

WHERE THE WILD THINGS ARE

STORY AND PICTURES BY MAURICE SENDAK

HARPER & ROW, PUBLISHERS

The Pacific Northwest Ballet's Nutcracker was staged in 1983 and filmed for movie theatres in 1986 as *Nutcracker: The Motion Picture*. The piece showcased sets and costumes by Sendak and this version of the ballet portrayed some of the darker aspects of E. T. A. Hoffmann's original story. Much of that flavor came from Sendak's imagination. This watercolor-on-paper illustration was published in *The Nutcracker*, by E. T. A. Hoffman and Maurice Sendak, Crown Publishers, 1984. At auction this brought **$14,938**, which seems incredibly cheap for such gorgeous art.

Image courtesy Heritage Auctions

A sample of various *Wild Thing* preliminary sketches, pencil on paper, 1963: **$4,688** at auction.

Image courtesy Heritage Auctions

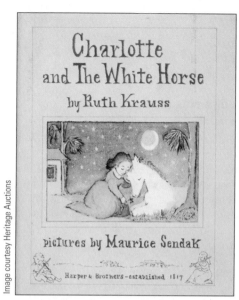

Charlotte and the White Horse

by Ruth Krauss, Maurice Sendak, illustrator, Harper's, 1955.

A rare Sendak illustrated book. **$62**

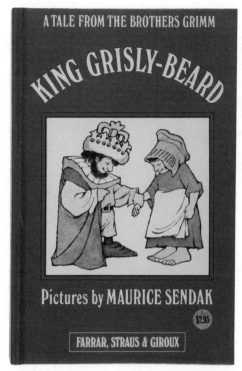

King Grisly-Beard

based on the Brothers Grimm story, illustrated by Sendak, New York: Farrar, Straus & Giroux, 1973.

First Edition. This generally near fine copy brought **$22** in an online auction.

Sendak worked with the brilliant playwright, screenwriter and National Medal of Arts recipient Tony Kushner on the book *Brundibar* (Michael Di Capua/Hyperion, 2003). Sendak and Kushner both signed this Frst Edition, first printing volume. **$138**.

Higglety Pigglety Pop! Or There Must Be More to Life

by Maurice Sendak, Harper & Row, 1979.

First paperback edition, signed by the author. **$92**

PICTURE BOOKS:

The Tiger Who Came To Tea
by Judith Kerr (1968):

What is it about this strange little book that is so appealing? The characters – Sophie, her mom and dad – react to a tiger's visit to their home with fairly mild alarm considering the situation. The tiger then eats and drinks them out of house and home; there isn't even any water left in the tap. The drawings, also by Kerr, are pleasingly lovely yet the undertone is dark. It comes as no surprise to learn that the author and her family escaped Nazi Germany when she was a child. Created as a bedtime story for her daughter, this is a book that is worth a look and that clearly understands children.

Blueberries for Sal
by Robert McCloskey (1948):

The author wrote so many that it's hard to choose, yet I'd say this is my favorite McCloskey book of all. The drawings so evocative of the time and place, the story so sweet and pleasurable. The idea of a mom and a toddler and a black bear and her cub getting their lines – and families – crossed was fascinating to our kid and will be to yours.

Pet Show by Ezra Jack Keats (1972):

It's hard to choose a favorite of his books – *A Snowy Day* must be read, of course – but it's *Pet Show* that makes me feel grateful for Ezra Jack Keats. *Pet Show* tells a tale on so many levels – the multicultural gathering, respect for the elderly, creative problem solving, a cat's independence – with Illustrations so evocative of a 1970s urban neighborhood.

Zen Shorts by Jon J. Muth (2005):

We and our daughter always really enjoyed this story, which is sort of like a summer day that leaves you sleepy and happy. Muth's big Bermuda Shorts-wearing panda, named Stillwater, befriends three children and gifts them with three stories in the form of short Zen parables that teach each of them valuable lessons.

"You brought me some cake!" said Stillwater. "That was very nice of you. Is it *your* birthday?" he asked.
"No," said Addy.
"It's not mine, either," said Stillwater. "But let me give you a gift for my uncle's birthday. I will tell you a story."

The Pink Refrigerator
by Tim Egan (2007):

Like Milo from *The Phantom Tollbooth*, Dodsworth is a couch potato, until the magic of the pink refrigerator comes into his life and transforms his motto from "Do as little as possible" to "Keep exploring." An absolute pleasure to read.

Milo's Hat Trick by John Agee (2001):

My family and I love everything by that Agee does, but this one is my personal favorite: a failed magician meets a bear with an amazing magic trick up his sleeve, which saves the magician's career. Just a great story with Agee's fantastically big, bold signature illustrations.

On Meadowview Street by Henry Cole (2007):

What a delightful find! Cole is a wonderful illustrator of many books, who occasionally – as here – will write his own text. The book begins with Caroline and her family moving into a house on Meadowview Street. Just as she is about to go look for the "meadow" she spots a flower as her dad is mowing the lawn. One thing leads to another – the dad sells the mower, they let their yard grow wild, add a tree and a pond, the neighbors follow suit – and soon there really is a meadow on Meadowview street and "a home for everyone."

Toot and Puddle by Holly Hobbie (1997):

Holly Hobbie has come a long way from the girl in the blue bonnet and gifts us with one of the greatest friendship stories ever told. Toot the traveler and Puddle the homebody are friends no matter what and this book teaches adults and kids alike so much about healthy friendship, not to mention that the illustrations are simply stunning.

Flotsam by David Wiesner (2006):

Truly a one-of-a-kind book from a one-of-a-kind talent. Told just through pictures, with no words, Weisner's detailed illustrations tell the wondrous tale of a boy who finds a camera on the beach and, in picking it up, becomes part of a network of children – and a fantastical undersea world – linked by the photos each takes of themselves over a span of time. One to re-visit over and over.

Kitten's First Full Moon by Kevin Henkes (2004):

We were introduced to the wonderful world of Kevin Henkes via the stunningly rich illustrations of this story about a kitten who mistakes a full moon for a bowl of milk. Henkes makes it all the more nostalgic through his masterful use of black and white. A playful, timeless, simple and well-crafted tale.

Miss Nelson is Missing by Harry Allard, illustrated by James Marshall (1997):

A laugh-out-loud story with Marshall's simple, vaudevillian drawings. Sweet, beautiful Miss Nelson is fed up with the bad behavior of the children of Room 207. Suddenly, she's gone and the mean, ugly Viola Swamp shows up. She whips the children into shape and finally Miss Nelson returns. Something is strange here, though, but Miss Nelson will never tell…

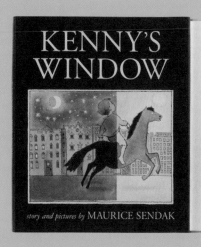

Kenny's Window

by Maurice Sendak, New York: Harper Collins, 1984.

Signed by the author on the half-title page. **$106**

Image courtesy Heritage Auctions

Some Swell Pup or Are You Sure You Want a Dog?

by Sendak and Matthew Margolis, New York: Farrar, Straus and Giroux, 1976

Not everything from Sendak is cost prohibitive. This First Edition of a relatively obscure Sendak project sold for **$15** at auction.

Image courtesy Heritage Auctions

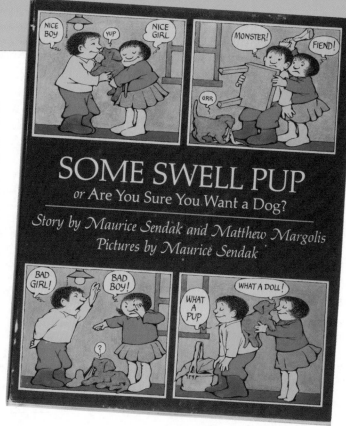

Bears

by Ruth Krause, Maurice Sendak, illustrator, New York: Harper Collins, 2005.

First Sendak illustrated edition, signed by Sendak. **$85**

Image courtesy Heritage Auctions

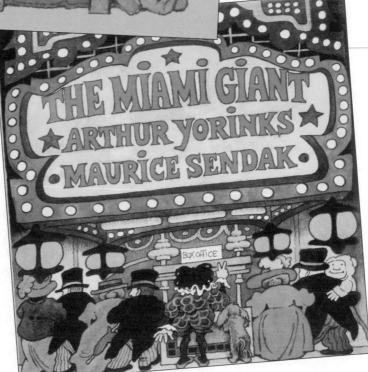

The Miami Giant

by Arthur Yorinks, Maurice Sendak, illustrator, Michael di Capua/HarperCollins, 1995.

First Edition signed by Sendak. **$53**

Image courtesy Heritage Auctions

Brooklyn Pops Up

Brooklyn Public Library, Maurice Sendak, contributor, New York: Simon & Schuster, 2000.

First Edition, second printing. A rarity, but still possible to find at reasonable prices for the Sendak die-hard. **$69**

Image courtesy Heritage Auctions

In the Night Kitchen

by Maurice Sendak, Harper & Row, 1970.

A fair price for a signed copy of this classic is somewhere north of **$60**, depending on the day and who's buying. Certainly the most favorite Sendak book (apologies to *Where the Wild Things Are*) in our house; so wonderfully rich, entertaining, inscrutable and infinitely interpretable.

Image courtesy Heritage Auctions

The Bee-Man of Orn

by Frank R. Stockton, illustrated by Maurice Sendak, New York, Harper & Row, 1986.

Later reprint edition, **$28** at auction.

We are All in the Dumps with Jack and Guy

by Maurice Sendak, Michael di Capua Books/Harper Collins, 1993.

First Edition, in near fine condition, expect to pay in the range of **$40** at auction.

Maurice Sendak, illustrator, William Blake, Poems from *William Blake's Songs of Innocence*, London: The Bodley Head, 1967: First and only printing of an edition limited to 275 copies for presentation at Christmas, printed for the publisher by the Stellar Press. Like so many of Sendak's post-Wild Things books, this is a rarity and hard to find. At auction this copy brought **$2,250**.

MAURICE SENDAK

A grouping of Sendak signed posters and art prints includes works for the Book Festival on Fifth Avenue (New York 1998) and a "Maurice Sendak" poster (1990). The grouping brought **$1,195** at auction.

Image courtesy Heritage Auctions

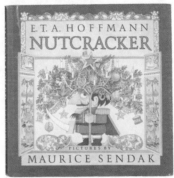

Three book illustrated by Maurice Sendak, including: *Hector Protector*, 1965; E. T. A. Hoffmann, *Nutcracker*, 1984 and *The Cunning Little Vixen* by Rudolf Tesnohlidek, 1985. All Frst Editions in very good condition. A bargain at **$56** in an online auction.

Image courtesy Heritage Auctions

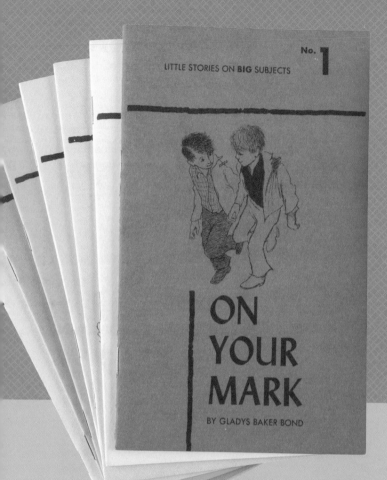

Seven Little Stories on Big Subjects

by Gladys Baker Bond, Maurice Sendak, illustrator, New York: Anti-Defamation League, 1955.

A complete set of seven rare booklets published by the Anti-Defamation League, each illustrated by Sendak with cover art and a few line vignettes in the text. The stories deal with various conflicts and situations that a young school child might face and how to handle them without getting physical. Including: #1 *On Your Mark*, #2 *Jacob's Friendliest Town*, #3 *The Crankiest Man On Main Street*, #4 *Down The Old Bear Trail*, #5 *Johnny Red Feather*, #6 *Lonesome Feet*, and #7 *The Secret*. A wonderful, rarely seen Sendak item. **$1,000**

Image courtesy Heritage Auctions

Sendak's first pop-up book, *Mommy?*, with Arthur Yorinks and Matthew Reinhart (Michael Di Capua Books and Scholastic, 2006) shown here in fine condition, is a rarity and will bring in the range of **$85** at auction.

Image courtesy Heritage Auctions

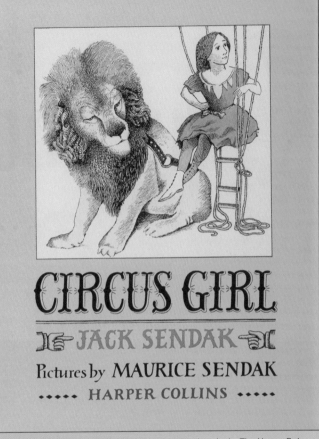

Sendak published two books with his older brother Jack: *The Happy Rain* (1956) and *Circus Girl* (1957). This copy of *Circus Girl* was published by Harper Collins in 1985 and is signed by Maurice Sendak. **$81**

Image courtesy Heritage Auctions

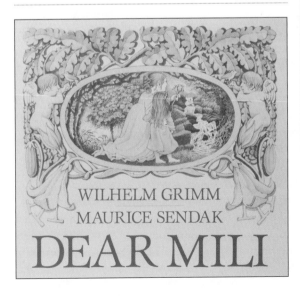

Dear Mili

by Wilhelm Grimm, Maurice Sendak, illustrator, Farrar, Straus and Giroux, 1988.

First Sendak illustrated edition, first printing, signed by Sendak. A good auction buy at **$81**.

Image courtesy Heritage Auctions

THE GOOD DOCTOR

There is no other children's writer that was as consistently brilliant, intuitive and innovative as Theodor Seuss Geisel, or as generations of admirers lovingly came to know him, Dr. Seuss. We all are familiar with his classic works and we all have a particular favorite. Seuss is timeless, possessing an innate ability to reach into a child's heart and do what may be the most important thing of all: make them laugh.

It was through laughter – whether in the form of his zany, logically illogical artwork or his incredible, simple and simultaneously complex rhymes – that Seuss made sense of the worlds he created, and what worlds they were. Across almost 50 books, in a career that spanned more than half a century and results in more than 200 million books sold, in dozens of languages, and countless cartoons and merchandizing tie-ins, Dr. Seuss became an icon, a verb, and a ubiquitous presence in the childhoods of the last three generations, and he's now working on a fourth.

Quick, name your favorite Seuss book. Chances are about five titles rushed into your head in quick succession.

When Seuss passed in September of 1991, the *New York Times* called him the "Modern Mother Goose," a designation that is hard to quibble with. Seuss produced a visual vernacular all his own, one that was specific to the stories, lessons and characters he was presenting us.

Can we point to a most famous book from the good doctor? Hardly. We can point to a handful of them, but for every one we name here, there are two more just as good. Not only that, Seuss's brilliance remained consistent from end-to-end. He wrote *The Cat in the Hat, The Cat in the Hat Come Back, Green Eggs and Ham, The Lorax, Oh The Places You'll Go, Horton Hears A Who, How The Grinch Stole Christmas, Yertle The Turtle, The Sneetches, Scrambled Eggs Super, If I Ran The Circus, And To Think I Saw It On Mulberry Street…* The list is deep and long.

Seuss was already quite famous and well along the path when he was asked to write *The Cat In The Hat* in 1957, arguably his most famous book, and the one that made him a household name. A direct response to the *Dick and Jane* reading primers of the day, using a limited vocabulary, Seuss penned the story of a lanky beanpole of a cat in a huge red hat who shows up at the house of Sally and her unnamed brother on a rainy day and who, along with his two creepy sidekicks – Thing 1 and Thing 2 – demolish the house and terrorize the poor fish before ultimately, in the moments before the children's mother shows back up, put everything neatly back in place. The effect is hysterical, terrifying and absurd. The result of the book was a complete paradigm shift in books aimed at beginning readers, and one that carries weight to this day. Seuss proved, beyond a shadow of a doubt, that books for the earliest readers could be fun, funny and instructive, not pedantic and repetitive like those he sought to replace.

To collectors, Seuss is always attractive, and when it comes to First Editions of his work, the older and more famous the book, the more you can expect to pay. First Editions of his biggest books – *Cat In The Hat, Cat In The Hat Comes Back, Green Eggs and Ham* – can run you as much as a few thousand dollars. The rest of the prices will be anywhere from $50 to $100 depending on condition and issue. A signature is always worth a bit more, as is an inscription or an original drawing, though quite rare.

There is not a tremendous amount of original Seuss art on the market these days, minus many specialty sketches he did of *The Cat,* or a creature of some kind, so if you had your heart set on a piece of original art from *Horton Hatches An Egg,* or *Hop on Pop,* you might want to re-think it. They just aren't out there in large supply, and what does show up on rare occasion will go for a premium, usually several thousand dollars.

It is worth remarking, however, that it's quite possible – if pricey – to get original animation cels from *How the Grinch Stole Christmas*, animated by the legendary Chuck Jones. Expect to pay anywhere from $750 up to $4,000+, depending on the scene and the image. While not expressly work from the hand of Dr. Seuss, the animation had his involvement from day one and was unanimously approved by him.

There is much to love and appreciate about Dr. Seuss. Fortunately for all of us, his books are infinitely readable, timeless and charming. You don't have to be a hardcore collector to amass a sizable grouping of Seuss books, in fact it can be done without spending a huge amount. You just have to be someone who loves the work and wants to own it so it's there to read when you desire. As far as I can tell, that's every single one of us.

Horton Hears a Who!

By Dr. Seuss, Random House, New York, 1954.

First Edition, first printing. This copy brought **$300** at auction. The delightful story of compassionate Horton, those who would break his spirit and tell him how wrong he is and his persistence in believing that all beings, no matter how small, are worthy of love and protection.

Image courtesy Justin Benttinen/ PBA Galleries.

Green Eggs and Ham

by Dr. Seuss, 1960.

First London edition, this prime copy brought **$938** at auction. This book is clearly one of the greats from the good doctor and easily in the top five of his best loved and most-widely read works. The tale of the Sam-I-Am wearing down the unnamed main character, to the point where he tries Green Eggs and Ham just to get rid of Sam-I-Am, and ends up enjoying them, never gets old, nor do the tour de force illustrations.

Image courtesy Justin Benttinen/PBA Galleries

Green Eggs
and Ham
for Sarah.....

Dr. Seuss

Would you like them
in a house?
Would you like them
with a mouse?

I do not like them in a box.
I do not like them with a fox.
I do not like them in a house.
I do not like them with a mouse.
I do not like them here or there.
I do not like them anywhere.
I do not like green eggs and ham.
I do not like them, Sam-I-am.

31

"Oh dear!" said the cat.

"You did not like our game . . .

Oh dear.

What a shame!

What a shame!

What a shame!"

53

The Cat In The Hat

by Dr. Seuss, Random House, New York, 1957.

First Edition and a nice copy of this classic icon of 20th-century children's literature, the first Dr. Seuss book specifically targeted for beginning readers and the one that established him as a household name and kicked off the very popular and influential Beginner Books series in spectacular fashion. **$2,400** at auction in this condition.

Image courtesy Justin Benttinen/PBA Galleries

Signed color Cat in The Hat sketch

A 6" x 9" book page featuring a printed image of Seuss' most popular creation, The Cat in The Hat. Alongside it is an image Seuss himself added in ink. Seuss sketches can be found and had at relatively inexpensive prices, but a quality image of The Cat is going to cost a bit. This one went for **$906** at auction.

Image courtesy of Heritage Auctions

The Cat in the Hat Comes Back

by Dr. Seuss, Beginner Books/Random House, New York, 1958.

First Edition, first printing. The famed cat is back in the follow-up to Seuss's masterpiece, *The Cat In The Hat*. A great one, no doubt, though we can remember Thing 1 and Thing 2 making us feel quite nervous in our youth with their decidedly wheels-off behavior. **$120**

Image courtesy Justin Benttinen/PBA Galleries

Original ink-and-marker drawing signed by Dr. Seuss. **$2,150**.

Image courtesy of Heritage Auctions

BOOKS FOR VERY YOUNG READERS:

Eric Carle

"Slowly,
Slowly,
Slowly,"
said the Sloth

Foreword by Jane Goodall

"Slowly, Slowly, Slowly," said the Sloth
by Eric Carle (2002):

This tale of the sloth, perfectly rendered by Carle, stands out to me among his many perfect books. The sloth, comfortable with just who he is no matter what anyone says, answers his detractors and sticks up for himself in an articulate and calm fashion, something we can all take a lesson from.

Chicka Chicka Boom Boom
by Bill Martin Jr. and John Archambault,
illustrated by Lois Ehlert (1989):

Toddler jazz, that's what this book is. The angular, smart illustrations match the bouncy rhymes. Toddlers learn their ABCs and 123s, acquire rhythmic sensibilities, and will want to read this over and over and over.

10 Minutes Till Bedtime
by Peggy Rathmann (1998):

One of those books of few words that begs to be "read" again and again, since each time the pictures yield a new discovery. The clever story of a boy's bedtime warnings from his father, during which the boy's pet hamster leads a family reunion/house tour of sorts, which they are barely able to pull off and still get to bed on time, is endlessly entertaining!

The Runaway Bunny by Margaret Wise Brown, illustrated by Clement Hurd (1942):

This book is from the same team that created *Goodnight Moon*. I love the back-and-forth switch between black-and-white and color illustrations as coupled with the gentle, imaginative repartee between the Mother Bunny and the Little Bunny. In all, this is just about the perfect book.

The Nutshell Library
by Maurice Sendak (1962):

This small-sized collection, secure within its own box, is perfect for young children and has always been my mom's choice for a new baby gift. Four different volumes, four distinct stories, all vintage Sendak. How can you go wrong?

Miffy Says "I Love You!" by Dick Bruna (2004):

Dutch artist Bruna created Miffy the bunny for his son in 1955. Today he runs a Miffy empire. Doesn't matter which book you choose, what I love most about Miffy books is they are simple and sweet, created in a minimalist style and written directly to the very young.

Photo courtesy Meserve-Kunhardt Foundation

Pat the Bunny
by Dorothy Kunhardt (1940):

This is the classic new baby gift and was the first of its kind "touch-and-feel" book. Simple directions lead kids to make simple and delightful tactile discoveries. My daughter always like to "feel Daddy's scratchy beard" in the book because it was the same in real life.

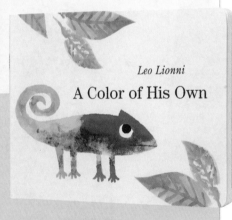

Leo Lionni
A Color of His Own

A Color of His Own
by Leo Lionni (1975):

This little book is the seemingly simple tale of a chameleon searching for his identity. Along the way we learn lessons about colors, animals, identity and friendship. The vivid watercolors for which Lionni became known are such a pleasure for young eyes that it's no wonder he won four Caldecott Medals, and not even for this book!

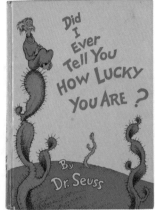

Did I Ever Tell You How Lucky You Are?
by Dr. Seuss, Random House, New York, 1973.

First Edition, first printing. Perfect antidote for readers feeling blue. **$50**

There's a Wocket in my Pocket!
by Dr. Seuss, Random House, New York, 1974.

First Edition. **$100** in an online auction.

So Many Bunnies
by Rick Walton, illustrated by Paige Miglio (1998):

The intricately detailed illustrations make this simple counting and ABC book shine. Mother Rabbit tucks all her 26 children into bed and we learn each of their names, where they sleep and the alphabet at the same time. Totally addictive!

Great Big Schoolhouse
by Richard Scarry (1969):

Similar to a graphic novel, there's something going on all over the page. The vaudevillian hi-jinx of Scarry's lovable, anthropomorphized characters – from Huckle the Cat to Lowly Worm – are strangely inappropriate on one hand, with runaway cars and thieving gorillas, yet somehow everything still works out in the end and it's a ton of fun.

Scrambled Eggs Super

by Dr. Seuss, New York: Random House, 1953.

First Edition of this absolute masterpiece. This is some of Seuss's most clever drawing and rhyming, even if its genius is somewhat under-appreciated by some modern readers. *Scrambled Eggs Super* was a staple in our house in the early years of our daughter's life and one of the first of his books that we read that unfolded the true scope of his brilliance beyond his staple titles. We have to say this book is a sleeper to take the top spot in our list of Seuss's greatest works – just sayin'. A very good buy at auction for **$256**.

Image courtesy Heritage Auctions

Dr. Seuss's Sleep Book

by Dr. Seuss, New York: Random House, 1962.

First Edition, a better than very good copy. A warning printed inside the book says it all: "This book is to be read in bed." **$125**.

Image courtesy Heritage Auctions

1756/2500   Dr. Seuss

The Art of Dr. Seuss Illustration Portfolio 3
Limited Edition #1756/2500 (The Chase Group)

Though his 60+ children's books are often best remembered for their imaginative characters, inspired rhyme and creative use of meter, it was Dr. Seuss's skill as an illustrator that brought them fully to life. This set of five color prints features artwork from *Fox in Socks, The Cat in the Hat Comes Back, How The Grinch Stole Christmas, One Fish Two Fish Red Fish Blue Fish,* and *Yertle the Turtle* and brought **$98** in an online auction.

Image courtesy Heritage Auctions

❝ *Fox in Socks* by Dr. Seuss. This is the book I still read with my son. He can hear it 5,000 times and never get tired. And let's be honest, you still never see that ending coming. This is my childhood in book form. Viva la tongue-twisting fox. **❞**

BRAD MELTZER is the bestselling author of the *Ordinary People Change the World Series*, including the books *I Am Abraham Lincoln* and *I Am Rosa Parks*. He lives in Florida.

Photo courtesy Eric Ogden

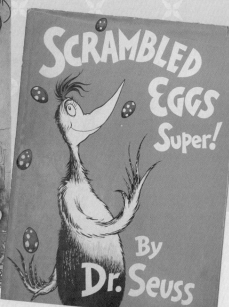

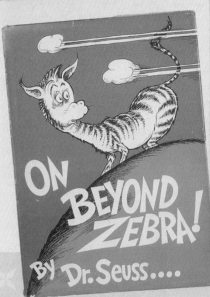

Marvin K. Mooney Will You Please Go Now!

By Dr. Seuss, Random House, New York, 1972.

First Edition, first printing. **$180**.

Image courtesy of Justin Benttinen/PBA Galleries

Lot of Six Books by Dr. Seuss

Including: *The 500 Hats of Bartholomew Cubbins*, New York: The Vanguard Press, 1938, a later printing of the First Edition; *The King's Stilts*, New York: Random House, 1939; *McElligot's Pool*, New York: Random House, 1947, likely a First Edition; *Scrambled Eggs Super!*, New York: Random House, 1953; *Horton Hears a Who!*, New York: Random House, 1954 and *On Beyond Zebra!*, New York: Random House, 1955. This grouping went for **$2,390**, making us, along with thousands of others, very sad we didn't take better care of our own copies! Even if they were not First Editions, rare Seuss is always popular with buyers of all levels. A grouping of later editions of these books would more than likely run you a few hundred dollars — well worth it, in our estimation.

Image courtesy Heritage Auctions

And to Think I Saw It On Mulberry Street
by Dr. Seuss, Vanguard Press, New York, 1937.

First Edition, first issue – with boy on front cover of volume and dust jacket in white shorts (versus blue shorts of later issues) – of Seuss's timeless first book. Hard to believe this books is almost 80 years old. This one brought **$1,920** at auction.

Image courtesy Justin Benttinen/PBA Galleries

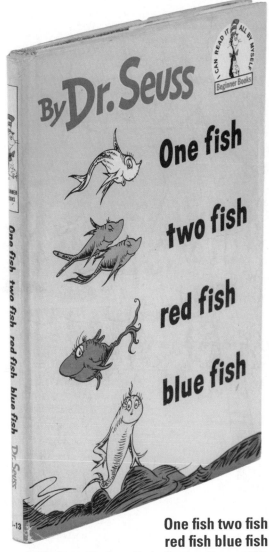

Yertle the Turtle and Other Stories
by Dr. Seuss, Random House, New York, 1958.

First Edition, first printing. **$156** at auction. The story of Yertle is a classic; Yertle is "the King of all I see, but I don't see enough and that's the trouble with me." His tyranny over the other turtles, however, is overthrown by the turtle, Mack, with questions and a well-timed burp.

Image courtesy Justin Benttinen/PBA Galleries

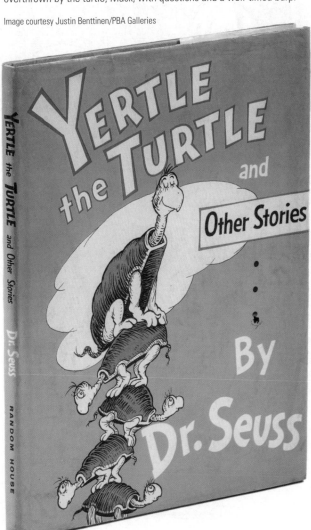

One fish two fish red fish blue fish
by Dr. Seuss, Beginner Books/Random House, 1960.

First Edition, first printing with the correct jacket blurbs and title listings; a book so many of us remember reading as we first started putting words together. **$120**

Image courtesy Justin Benttinen/PBA Galleries

This way! Step right in! This way, lad[ies]
My Side Show starts here in the first [
When you see what goes on, you'll s[ee]
Half the great circus the Circus McG[
Here on Stage One, from the Ocean [
Is a sight most amazing—a walrus na[
Who can stand on *one whisker*, this v[
On the top of five balls! Two for to[
It's a marvelous trick, if I say so my[

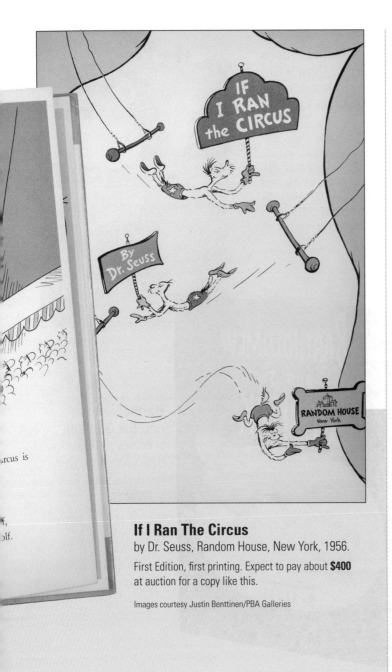

Oh, the Thinks You Can Think!
by Dr. Seuss, Random House, New York, 1975.

First Edition, publisher's binding. The mind's potential and the unlimited "thinks" one can think are celebrated in this salute to endless possibilities and dreams our imaginations can create. This edition is in generally good condition and sold for **$89**.

Images courtesy Heritage Auctions

If I Ran The Circus
by Dr. Seuss, Random House, New York, 1956.

First Edition, first printing. Expect to pay about **$400** at auction for a copy like this.

Images courtesy Justin Benttinen/PBA Galleries

The Lorax
by Dr. Seuss, Random House, New York, 1971.

First Edition, first printing. This book is one of the very first to directly assess the impact of pollution and greed on the environment, and it's still a very powerful testament to the devastation humans are wreaking on the planet. It also directly reflects the age in which it was written, the early 1970s, when environmental movements against pollution and trash kicked into full swing. *The Lorax* was made into an animated musical in 2012, which, while popular with kids, radically changed the ending – something we do not agree with – with The Lorax coming back, after he has left and the people have realized the error of their ways and telling them that they "have done well." Where is the lesson and the responsibility in that, we ask? It was the finality of The Lorax's final act of "lifting himself by the seat of his pants" through a hole in the sky that makes this such a devastating, beautiful and powerful book. This First Edition was available online for **$59.99**.

Image courtesy eBay, seller neufeld_holdings.

Oh, the Places You'll Go!
by Dr. Seuss, Random House, New York, 1990.

The last book published by Dr. Seuss offers hope to all who forge their own path: "Will you succeed? Yes, you will indeed. (98 3/4% guaranteed.)" Available for between **$6** to **$15** online, depending on condition.

Images courtesy Random House

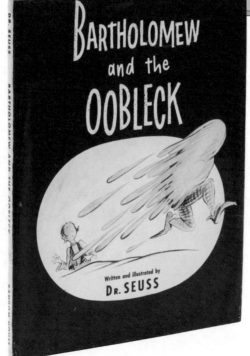

Bartholomew and the Oobleck
by Dr. Seuss, Random House, New York, 1949.

First Edition; **$360** at auction.

Image courtesy of Justin Benttinen/ PBA Galleries.

McElliot's Pool

by Dr. Seuss, Random House, New York, 1947.

First Edition, first printing. **$360**

Image courtesy Justin Benttinen/PBA Galleries

I Had Trouble in getting to Solla Sollew

by Dr. Seuss, Random House, New York, 1965.

First Edition, first printing. A copy in good condition like this will likely run you in the range of **$200**.

Image courtesy Justin Benttinen/PBA Galleries

How The Grinch Stole Christmas

by Dr. Seuss, Random House, New York, 1957.

First Editon, first printing. Signed by Seuss on the verso of the dedication page. A memorable story made even more so by the transcendent 1966 TV special with the Grinch voiced by Boris Karloff. **$3,500**

Image courtesy Heritage Auctions

Then the *Whos*, young and old, would sit down to a feast.
And they'd feast! *And they'd feast!*
And they'd FEAST!
FEAST!
FEAST!
FEAST!
They would feast on *Who*-pudding, and rare *Who*-roast-beast
Which was something the Grinch couldn't stand in the least!

Dr. Seuss's *How the Grinch Stole Christmas* Grinch production cel signed by Chuck Jones (Warner Brothers, 1966): An original 12-field, hand-painted production cel of the Grinch looking down at poor Max the dog, hand-signed by Jones, over a production background. Backgrounds from this special are considered rare. This one is spectacular. From the Chuck Jones Collection, this brought **$4,780** at auction.

Image courtesy Heritage Auctions

Dr. Seuss's *How the Grinch Stole Christmas* Cindy Lou Who production cel (MGM Studios, 1966)

An original 12-field, hand-painted production cel of little Cindy Lou Who, from one of the most beloved holiday specials of all time. Hand-signed by Chuck Jones. **$1,793**

Image courtesy Heritage Auctions

An exceptional hand-painted studio publicity cel, used for gifts and studio promotion, features the Grinch, Max and Cindy Lou. **$1,015**

Image courtesy Heritage Auctions

Dr. Seuss's *How the Grinch Stole Christmas* Grinch Production Cels (MGM, 1966)

Three 12-field hand-painted production cels (numbered 38, 39, and 51) of the Grinch slithering across the floor to steal toys and Christmas trees. Sequences of production cels are rarely seen. At **$777**, it seems like a good buy to us at auction.

Image courtesy Heritage Auctions

The Grinch in action captured in this beautiful production cel signed by Chuck Jones from *How the Grinch Stole Christmas*. A grand moment from a holiday masterpiece. **$2,150**

Image courtesy Heritage Auctions

The Grinch sews a Santa Clause outfit with the help of Max, his good-hearted yet puzzled dog. The signed cel realized **$3,465** at auction.

Image courtesy Heritage Auctions

This production cel provides a nice close-up of a happy-looking Grinch, the star of Dr. Seuss's *How the Grinch Stole Christmas*. Signed by animator/director Chuck Jones, this prize realized **$2,270** at auction a few years ago. Today you can expect to pay more for the image measuring approximately 3" by 8".

Image courtesy Heritage Auctions

Appendix

THE NEWBERRY MEDAL

Awarded annually by the Association for Library Service to Children (ALSC), a division of the American Library Association (ALA), the Newbery Medal was the first of its kind. The award is fittingly named after John Newbery, an 18th century British bookseller, who first conceived of the idea of publishing books for and marketing them to children. Each year since 1922, the award is presented to "the most distinguished American children's book of the previous year." Despite the plethora of children's book awards today, it remains the most prestigious.

The following are winners of the Newberry Medal:

2015: *The Crossover*, written by Kwame Alexander

2014: *Flora & Ulysses: The Illuminated Adventures* by Kate DiCamillo

2013: *The One and Only Ivan* by Katherine Applegate

2012: *Dead End in Norvelt* by Jack Gantos

2011: *Moon over Manifest* by Clare Vanderpool

2010: *When You Reach Me* by Rebecca Stead

2009: *The Graveyard Book* by Neil Gaiman, illus. by Dave McKean

2008: *Good Masters! Sweet Ladies! Voices from a Medieval Village* by Laura Amy Schlitz

2007: *The Higher Power of Lucky* by Susan Patron, illus. by Matt Phelan

2006: *Criss Cross* by Lynne Rae Perkins

2005: *Kira-Kira* by Cynthia Kadohata

2004: *The Tale of Despereaux: Being the Story of a Mouse, a Princess, Some Soup, and a Spool of Thread* by Kate DiCamillo

2003: *Crispin: The Cross of Lead* by Avi

2002: *A Single Shard* by Linda Sue Park

2001: *A Year Down Yonder* by Richard Peck

2000: *Bud, Not Buddy* by Christopher Paul Curtis

1999: *Holes* by Louis Sachar

1998: *Out of the Dust* by Karen Hesse

1997: *The View from Saturday* by E.L. Konigsburg

1996: *The Midwife's Apprentice* by Karen Cushman

1995: *Walk Two Moons* by Sharon Creech

1994: *The Giver* by Lois Lowry

1993: *Missing May* by Cynthia Rylant

1992: *Shiloh* by Phyllis Reynolds Naylor

1991: *Maniac Magee* by Jerry Spinelli

1990: *Number the Stars* by Lois Lowry

1989: *Joyful Noise: Poems for Two Voices* by Paul Fleischman

1988: *Lincoln: A Photobiography* by Russell Freedman

1987: *The Whipping Boy* by Sid Fleischman

1986: *Sarah, Plain and Tall* by Patricia MacLachlan

1985: *The Hero and the Crown* by Robin McKinley

1984: *Dear Mr. Henshaw* by Beverly Cleary

1983: *Dicey's Song* by Cynthia Voigt

1982: *A Visit to William Blake's Inn: Poems for Innocent and Experienced Travelers* by Nancy Willard

1981: *Jacob Have I Loved* by Katherine Paterson

1980: *A Gathering of Days: A New England Girl's Journal, 1830-1832* by Joan W. Blos

1979: *The Westing Game* by Ellen Raskin

1978: *Bridge to Terabithia* by Katherine Paterson

1977: *Roll of Thunder, Hear My Cry* by Mildred D. Taylor

1976: *The Grey King* by Susan Cooper

1975: *M. C. Higgins, the Great* by Virginia Hamilton

1974: *The Slave Dancer* by Paula Fox

1973: *Julie of the Wolves* by Jean Craighead George

1972: *Mrs. Frisby and the Rats of NIMH* by Robert C. O'Brien

1971: *Summer of the Swans* by Betsy Byars

1970: *Sounder* by William H. Armstrong

1969: *The High King* by Lloyd Alexander

1968: *From the Mixed-Up Files of Mrs. Basil E. Frankweiler* by E.L. Konigsburg

1967: *Up a Road Slowly* by Irene Hunt

1966: *I, Juan de Pareja* by Elizabeth Borton de Trevino

1965: *Shadow of a Bull* by Maia Wojciechowska

1964: *It's Like This, Cat* by Emily Neville

1963: *A Wrinkle in Time* by Madeleine L'Engle

1962: *The Bronze Bow* by Elizabeth George Speare

1961: *Island of the Blue Dolphins* by Scott O'Dell

1960: *Onion John* by Joseph Krumgold

1959: *The Witch of Blackbird Pond* by Elizabeth George Speare

1958: *Rifles for Watie* by Harold Keith

1957: *Miracles on Maple Hill* by Virginia Sorensen

1956: *Carry On, Mr. Bowditch* by Jean Lee Latham

1955: *The Wheel on the School* by Meindert DeJong

1954: *...And Now Miguel* by Joseph Krumgold

1953: *Secret of the Andes* by Ann Nolan Clark

1952: *Ginger Pye* by Eleanor Estes

1951: *Amos Fortune, Free Man* by Elizabeth Yates

1950: *The Door in the Wall* by Marguerite de Angeli

1949: *King of the Wind* by Marguerite Henry

1948: *The Twenty-One Balloons* by William Pène du Bois

1947: *Miss Hickory* by Carolyn Sherwin Bailey

1946: *Strawberry Girl* by Lois Lenski

1945: *Rabbit Hill* by Robert Lawson

1944: *Johnny Tremain* by Esther Forbes

1943: *Adam of the Road* by Elizabeth Janet Gray

1942: *The Matchlock Gun* by Walter Edmonds

1941: *Call It Courage* by Armstrong Sperry

1940: *Daniel Boone* by James Daugherty

1939: *Thimble Summer* by Elizabeth Enright

1938: *The White Stag* by Kate Seredy

1937: *Roller Skates* by Ruth Sawyer

1936: *Caddie Woodlawn* by Carol Ryrie Brink

1935: *Dobry* by Monica Shannon

1934: *Invincible Louisa: The Story of the Author of Little Women* by Cornelia Meigs

1933: *Young Fu of the Upper Yangtze* by Elizabeth Lewis

1932: *Waterless Mountain* by Laura Adams Armer

1931: *The Cat Who Went to Heaven* by Elizabeth Coatsworth

1930: *Hitty, Her First Hundred Years* by Rachel Field

1929: *The Trumpeter of Krakow* by Eric P. Kelly

1928: *Gay Neck, the Story of a Pigeon* by Dhan Gopal Mukerji

1927: *Smoky, the Cowhorse* by Will James

1926: *Shen of the Sea* by Arthur Bowie Chrisman

1925: *Tales from Silver Lands* by Charles Finger

1924: *The Dark Frigate* by Charles Hawes

1923: *The Voyages of Doctor Dolittle* by Hugh Lofting

1922: *The Story of Mankind* by Hendrik Willem van Loon

THE CALDECOTT MEDAL

On the heels of the institution of the Newbery Medal, many became concerned that the illustrators of children's books deserved the same honor and encouragement as the authors. The American Library Association (ALA) established a second medal, named for 19th-century illustrator Randolph J. Caldecott, who many consider the father of the modern picture book. In 1937 the first Caldecott Medal was awarded to the "the most distinguished American picture book for children."

The following are winners of the Caldecott Medal:

2015: *The Adventures of Beekle: The Unimaginary Friend*, illustrated and written by Dan Santat

2014: *Locomotive*, written and illustrated by Brian Floca

2013: *This Is Not My Hat*, written and illustrated by Jon Klassen

2012: *A Ball for Daisy* by Chris Raschka

2011: *A Sick Day for Amos McGee,* illustrated by Erin E. Stead, written by Philip C. Stead

2010: *The Lion & the Mouse* by Jerry Pinkney

2009: *The House in the Night*, illustrated by Beth Krommes; text by Susan Marie Swanson

2008: *The Invention of Hugo Cabret* by Brian Selznick

2007: *Flotsam* by David Wiesner

2006: *The Hello, Goodbye Window*, illustrated by Chris Raschka; text by Norton Juster

2005: *Kitten's First Full Moon* by Kevin Henkes

2004: *The Man Who Walked Between the Towers* by Mordicai Gerstein

2003: *My Friend Rabbit* by Eric Rohmann

2002: *The Three Pigs* by David Wiesner

2001: *So You Want to Be President?*, Illustrated by David Small; text by Judith St. George

2000: *Joseph Had a Little Overcoat* by Simms Taback

1999: *Snowflake Bentley*, Illustrated by Mary Azarian; text by Jacqueline Briggs Martin

1998: *Rapunzel* by Paul O. Zelinsky

1997: *Golem* by David Wisniewski

1996: *Officer Buckle and Gloria* by Peggy Rathmann

1995: *Smoky Night*, illustrated by David Diaz; text: Eve Bunting

1994: *Grandfather's Journey* by Allen Say

1993: *Mirette on the High Wire* by Emily Arnold McCully

1992: *Tuesday* by David Wiesner

1991: *Black and White* by David Macaulay

1990: *Lon Po Po: A Red-Riding Hood Story from China* by Ed Young

1989: *Song and Dance Man*, illustrated by Stephen Gammell; text: Karen Ackerman

1988: *Owl Moon*, illustrated by John Schoenherr; text: Jane Yolen

1987: *Hey, Al*, illustrated by Richard Egielski; text: Arthur Yorinks

1986: *The Polar Express* by Chris Van Allsburg

1985: *Saint George and the Dragon*, illustrated by Trina Schart Hyman; text: retold by Margaret Hodges

1984: *The Glorious Flight: Across the Channel* with Louis Bleriot by Alice & Martin Provensen

1983: *Shadow*, translated and illustrated by Marcia Brown; original text in French: Blaise Cendrars

1982: *Jumanji* by Chris Van Allsburg

1981: *Fables* by Arnold Lobel

1980: *Ox-Cart Man*, illustrated by Barbara Cooney; text: Donald Hall

1979: *The Girl Who Loved Wild Horses* by Paul Goble

1978: *Noah's Ark* by Peter Spier

1977: *Ashanti to Zulu: African Traditions*, illustrated by Leo & Diane Dillon; text: Margaret Musgrove

1976: *Why Mosquitoes Buzz in People's Ears*, illustrated by Leo & Diane Dillon; text: retold by Verna Aardema

1975: *Arrow to the Sun* by Gerald McDermott

1974: *Duffy and the Devil*, illustrated by Margot Zemach; retold by Harve Zemach

1973: *The Funny Little Woman*, illustrated by Blair Lent; text: retold by Arlene Mosel

1972: *One Fine Day*, retold and illustrated by Nonny Hogrogian

1971: *A Story A Story*, retold and illustrated by Gail E. Haley

1970: *Sylvester and the Magic Pebble* by William Steig

1969: *The Fool of the World and the Flying Ship*, illustrated by Uri Shulevitz; text: retold by Arthur Ransome

1968: *Drummer Hoff*, illustrated by Ed Emberley; text: adapted by Barbara Emberley

1967: *Sam, Bangs & Moonshine* by Evaline Ness

1966: *Always Room for One More*, illustrated by Nonny Hogrogian; text: Sorche Nic Leodhas, pseud. [Leclair Alger]

1965: *May I Bring a Friend?*, illustrated by Beni Montresor; text: Beatrice Schenk de Regniers

1964: *Where the Wild Things Are* by Maurice Sendak

1963: *The Snowy Day* by Ezra Jack Keats

1962: *Once a Mouse*, retold and illustrated by Marcia Brown

1961: *Baboushka and the Three Kings*, illustrated by Nicolas Sidjakov; text: Ruth Robbins

1960: *Nine Days to Christmas*, illustrated by Marie Hall Ets; text: Marie Hall Ets and Aurora Labastida

1959: *Chanticleer and the Fox*, illustrated by Barbara Cooney; text: adapted from Chaucer's *Canterbury Tales* by Barbara Cooney

1958: *Time of Wonder* by Robert McCloskey

1957: *A Tree Is Nice*, illustrated by Marc Simont; text: Janice Udry

1956: *Frog Went A-Courtin'*, illustrated by Feodor Rojankovsky; text: retold by John Langstaff

1955: *Cinderella, or the Little Glass Slipper*, illustrated by Marcia Brown; text: translated from Charles Perrault by Marcia Brown

1954: *Madeline's Rescue* by Ludwig Bemelmans

1953: *The Biggest Bear* by Lynd Ward

1952: *Finders Keepers*, illustrated by Nicolas, pseud. (Nicholas Mordvinoff); text: Will, pseud. [William Lipkind]

1951: *The Egg Tree* by Katherine Milhous

1950: *Song of the Swallows* by Leo Politi

1949: *The Big Snow* by Berta & Elmer Hader

1948: *White Snow, Bright Snow*, illustrated by Roger Duvoisin; text: Alvin Tresselt

1947: *The Little Island*, illustrated by Leonard Weisgard; text: Golden MacDonald, pseud for Margaret Wise Brown

1946: *The Rooster Crows* by Maude & Miska Petersham

1945: *Prayer for a Child*, illustrated by Elizabeth Orton Jones; text: Rachel Field

1944: *Many Moons*, illustrated by Louis Slobodkin; text: James Thurber

1943: *The Little House* by Virginia Lee Burton

1942: *Make Way for Ducklings* by Robert McCloskey

1941: *They Were Strong and Good*, by Robert Lawson

1940: *Abraham Lincoln* by Ingri & Edgar Parin d'Aulaire

1939: *Mei Li* by Thomas Handforth

1938: *Animals of the Bible, A Picture Book*, illustrated by Dorothy P. Lathrop; text: selected by Helen Dean Fish

Index